ANOTHER WAY OF PUTTING IT

By **Tim Jones** and

Jim Butterworth

Illustrations by **Corbin Hillam**

STANDARD
PUBLISHING
Cincinnati, Ohio

Permission to Copy

As you know, material is copyrighted to protect the author and pub-
lisher from loss of sales. Copying someone else's sheet music (or
musical tapes!) or handing out copies of student workbook pages
instead of buying your own is against the law. For a few of these skits,
however, you'd have to buy five or six copies of this book in order to
give each character a script. We don't want you to have to do that, so
we are hereby giving special permission to copy the skits in this book;
the pages are perforated to make this easier for you. But for one
church to buy a copy to the book and provide another group with
copies of a script, or to loan the entire book for that purpose, would of
course be an abuse of this special permission. We trust our buyers will
act accordingly.

Scripture quotes in this book are from the *Holy Bible: New
International Version,* © 1973, 1978, International Bible Society. Used
by permission of Zondervan Bible Publishers and the International
Bible Society.

Edited by Theresa C. Hayes

Library of Congress Cataloging-in-Publication Data

Butterworth, Jim, 1962-
      Another way of putting it / by Jim Butterworth and Tim Jones.
         p. cm.
      Cover subtitle: 20 short plays with a point.
      ISBN 0-87403-854-5
      1. Drama in Christian education. 2. Church work with youth.
I. Jones, Tim, 1959- . II. Title.
BV1534.4.B89 1991   91-7280
246'.7—dc20   CIP

Thanks!

To the original "Last Hour Players,"
Pelc, Herschel, Bucko, Roland, Greg, and Di,
and to Lisa, *die Liebe meines Lebens*.
—*Tim*

Special thanks to Mildred for her friendship,
Larry, Doug, and Jim for their inspiration,
and especially to my wife, Shannon,
who is a constant source of comedy,
inspiration, and love.
—*Jim*

Contents

Introduction

We are happy to present to you, *Another Way of Putting It*, a collection of our best skits. Each of these skits has been performed in countless youth-group meetings, church services, and at several large conventions, so you can certainly use them in a variety of circumstances. They can be presented with minimal props and costumes, although we have found that kids often have as much fun making preparations as they do presenting the skit!

Sometimes, drama can reach a place in us that no spoken word or song can touch. And while teaching is the main goal, these skits will entertain as well. We pray that your audience not only laughs at least once or twice, but also receives the message and takes it to heart. Of course, drama doesn't have to be funny to get the point across, but humor sure keeps things interesting!

You *could* present your message in song, by preaching, through sign language, or by spray painting it on the side of an overpass. Or, you can deliver your message with a dramatic skit, which is, *Another Way of Putting It*.

Have fun,
Jim and Tim

Adjective Salesman

Characters

Vendor, a street-smart hustler. Unable to morally justify what he does, but willing to do or say anything for a buck. Reluctantly acknowledges the creator.

Lisa, searching for meaning in her life, but not easily bamboozled.

Setting

A stadium, although the physical characteristics of a stadium never come into play. A chair, the characters' clothing, and the audience's imagination will suffice.

Props

Vendor outfit—white apron and cap

Vendor tray with the word, "Adjectives," clearly marked on the front.

Adjective Cards—various adjectives, including the ones referred to by the vendor, emblazoned on the front, large enough for audience to read.

Local team shirt or jacket for whatever sport is in season.

Spectator paraphernalia; binoculars, thermos bottle, whatever you choose.

Performance Tips

The more realistically the characters play their parts, the better the abstract concept of the play will come across.

Scene: *Lisa is sitting in ball park bleachers looking bored. Vendor enters, holding tray of unseen items.*

Vendor: Adjectives! Adjectives! Get your fresh adjectives!

Lisa: Oh, another vendor! First hot dogs, then peanuts, then *(realization)* adjectives? *(To vendor):* What do you mean, adjectives?

Vendor: Adjectives—you know—descriptive words, like "blue" or "checkered" or "glow-in-the-dark."

Lisa: Yes, I know what adjectives are. You mean you're actually selling them?

Vendor: Well, I can't just give them away. I've gotta make a living, you know. Do you know how expensive lettuce is these days? And not to mention . . . .

Lisa: No, you're missing the point. How could you possible *sell* adjectives? People use them every day, without having to buy them from everyone.

Vendor: Oh, I see what you're thinking. But, these aren't ordinary adjectives—these are life adjectives!

Lisa: What do you mean by, "life adjectives"?

Vendor: When you buy one of these babies from me, from that time forward, you are known by that word. It becomes the word that people use to describe you.

Lisa: I still don't quite follow.

Vendor: Well, let's see here. *(He begins to sort through his cards.)* Lemme give you an example. Let's see . . . okay . . . here's one of our biggest sellers *(he holds up "cool")*—cool. If you buy this adjective, others will know you, think of you and refer to you as "cool."

Lisa: What? That's all there is to being cool? Just buying the right adjective from you?

Vendor: Sure! Of course, I can't promise you that you will *be* cool; I just said people will *think* you are. Big difference!

Lisa: Right! Well, what is the price of these adjectives?

Vendor: They vary, depending on the nature of the adjective. *(Suddenly slips into his memorized sales pitch.)* But I assure you, ma'am, that all our top-of-the-line adjectives are reasonably priced to suit your shopping needs.

Lisa: Wow! Well, how much is "cool"?

Vendor *(Still in salesman voice):* An amazingly low price! For this sparkling new adjective, we merely ask that you give up your *(he coughs at the same time)* specialness. Would you like to sign on this dotted line now?

Lisa: Wait! I give up my what?

Vendor *(reluctantly):* Your specialness. But it's just a small price to pay for seeming cool! Fitting in with whatever group happens to be surrounding you, always knowing what to do to win favor *(big smile)*.

Lisa: Hmmm . . . everyone would know me as cool, huh?

Vendor: Cooler than an air-conditioned igloo! Is this a sale?

Lisa: But I lose my specialness!

Vendor *(evasively):* Well, really though . . . I mean, when you think about it, you're not exactly *losing*. You're actually . . . I mean *(pause)*. . . . Yes, I'm afraid so . . . you'd lose it all. Your special, unique, individual self, your own, one-of-a-kind personality—your contribution to the human picture—will be suppressed so you can become a part of the herd, a part of the in-crowd.

Lisa: Permanently?

Vendor: As long as you wear the adjective "cool," yes. Of course, it expires at death or when your life ends, whichever comes first.

Lisa *(looks confused):* Well, no one can fault you for not being honest. What other adjectives are you selling?

Vendor *(back in his salesman voice):* What else, you ask? Well, just wait 'til you see! We've got "famous," we've got "sophisticated," we've got "religious" . . . .

Lisa: Wait, slow down! Tell me about "famous."

Vendor: Oh, I'm sure that would interest you . . . .

Lisa: Oooh! Famous! That sends chills up and down my spine!

Vendor: No, that's the kid behind you. He spilled ice down your shirt. *(To imaginary kid):* Watch it, kid! Uh . . . where were we?

Lisa: Famous!

Vendor: Oh, yes, famous. Well, how would you like millions of people smiling at the mention of your name, posters of *you* on walls everywhere, kids tingling with excitement when they get to see *you* in person?

Lisa: Ooh, what a thought! Giving out autographs . . . staying in fancy hotel rooms . . . . I bet I'd always have a good parking space.

Vendor: Oh, you bet! *(Condescending salesman laugh.)*

Lisa: And the price?

Vendor: Hmmm?

Lisa: The price—what's the price?

Vendor: Oh, you worry too much about the cost of things! I mean, if you want it badly enough, any amount is worth it, right?

Lisa *(impatiently):* What's the price?

Vendor: Umm . . . relaxation.

Lisa: What do you mean, relaxation?

Vendor: Well, it's pretty simple. When you're famous, you've got to maintain your image. As long as someone's watching, you've got to perform—be the person they expect you to be. And you never know *when* others are watching—or if your close friends are real friends.

Lisa: Oooh, I really like to relax. What else do you have? Wait, didn't you say something about religious? Surely *that's* within my price range . . . .

Vendor: Oh yes! Religious— *(quieter)* looking.

Lisa: Religious-*looking?*

Vendor: Well, yes. As long as you live, you can walk down the street and people will stand in awe of how righteous you look. They'll even feel inferior because they're not as good as you appear. You'll have that glow of holiness about you.

Lisa: But will I really *be* righteous?

Vendor: Well, no, that's a different thing. I can't sell "righteousness." I sell, "religious-looking." Someone else bought "righteousness" for everyone, but it cost Him His life. And, most people don't even look into it.

Lisa: Well, if I'm not really good, what's the sense of looking that way? I'd have to give up my honesty!

Vendor: Hey, have you been reading my price tags? That is exactly what it costs to be religious-looking—your honesty. You pretend like you never make mistakes, like you never doubt, like you never have down times. If you want "religious-looking," you give up your honesty.

Lisa: Oh, how depressing! Isn't there anything in there I can afford? I've just gotta have an adjective!

Vendor *(starts sorting through):* Well, I don't know what to tell you. I've pretty much—*("genuine" pops up).*

Lisa: Hey, there's one I haven't seen—"genuine." Show me that one!

Vendor: Oh, it figures! This old thing? It's not worth selling.

Lisa: What's it cost?

Vendor *(sigh):* Well, nothing, but . . .

Lisa: Nothing?!

Vendor: Yeah, nothing. It's a freebie. "Genuine" is yours, when you give up trying to get other adjectives. When you stop chasing after something you're not, you're automatically "genuine."

Lisa: Wow! What a deal! It couldn't get much better than that!

Vendor: Well, yeah, it could. *(Pouting):* Even though *I* don't make a penny on this, it just so happens that with "genuine" you get a bonus adjective—"happy."

Lisa: A bonus?

Vendor: Yeah. Well, it's actually a manufacturer's rebate.

Lisa: What manufacturer?

Vendor: *The* Manufacturer—like of the universe—and us!

Lisa: Oh, *that* Manufacturer!

Vendor: I think His reasoning is, if you choose to be genuine, then you love truth. If you love truth, then you'll be happy. Something like, "Happy are those who hunger after what's right, 'cause they'll be satisfied."

Lisa: Makes sense! *(Realizes something.)* Wait, if you know these other adjectives cost a lot and yet don't bring happiness, how can you sell them?

Vendor *(defensively):* Hey! Hey! I gotta make a living!

Lisa: Sounds to me like you're making a killing!

Curtain

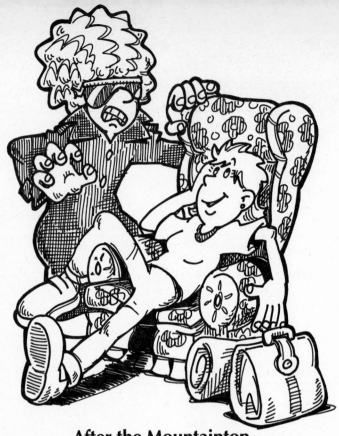

After the Mountaintop

Characters

Lisa, young Christian, (the same age as your intended audience) who is fired up from a week of camp (or revival, retreat, or whatever has occurred in your area).

Demon, sarcastic, hateful, clever

Setting

Lisa's bedroom or living room

Props/Costumes

Do something to the demon to make him appear odd; a fright wig, green face makeup, extraordinarily long fingernails. Don't make him comical; the more natural, the scarier.

Lisa is wearing home-from-camp clothes

Easy chair

Bible
Sleeping bag
Suitcase
TV, *TV Guide*
Radio
Radio transmitter, to be carried by the demon. May be a
    portable phone, a play phone, a wristwatch (à la Dick
    Tracy) or a shoe phone (à la Maxwell Smart).

Performance Tips

Lisa is in a chair, center stage, not quite facing front. The
demon remains behind her the entire time and she hears him
only when he speaks directly in her ear. Even then, she
responds as if to a voice in her head. In other words, Lisa nei-
ther sees nor hears the demon, although the audience does.

Scene: *Lisa comes in with Bible, sleeping bag, and suitcase. She
plops down in the chair, sighs happily, and smiles. Demon
comes slinking in behind.*

Lisa: What a great week of camp!

Demon *(mocking):* What a great week of camp! Blecch!

Lisa: I feel so close to God!

Demon: Oh, shut up! I'm gonna lose my lunch! Maybe break-
    fast, too! And it just doesn't taste as good the second time
    around.

Lisa: So many Scriptures seemed to jump out at me!

Demon: Those were crickets that were hiding in your Bible.

Lisa: I'm on a mountaintop!

Demon: Yeah, and the high altitude is making you dizzy.

Lisa: And I got so close to so many people.

Demon: Hey, that's called "crowded facilities," toots.

Lisa: And to think I almost didn't go. I can see the devil was
    really working on me.

Demon *(sarcastically):* Oh, so you noticed me! That's beautiful! I'm touched. I'm also nauseous. *(Buzzer sounds.)* Oh, no! It's the main office. *(Buzz.)* Oh oh! How am I gonna explain this one? *(Buzz.)* Yikes! *(He picks up the receiver.)*

(While he speaks to the main office, Lisa rests in the chair. She can reminiscing about camp with a smile on her face and her eyes shut, or she may casually peruse the papers in her Bible.)

Demon: What? I mean, yes, your hatefulness . . . *(He reacts as if to a loud voice on the other end.)* Yes, I'm sorry . . . . Yes. . . . How was I to know? She was sitting with her friends . . . They were shaping little animals out of chewing gum 'till halfway through the sermon . . . You should've seen the neat little anteater she made. It—what? No, of course not, sir, nevermind. Well, it was that fourth verse of "I Have Decided to Follow Jesus" that did it. . . . Hey, chill out! Oh yeah, you can't down there. . . . Well, I'm sure it's only a fling. . . . Just a shallow, superficial thing; it'll pass! I promise! I'll have her mind on worldly things in no time! Sure, count on me, your loathesomeness. *(Looks insulted.)* Yeah, same to you! *(He hangs up.)* His breath stinks even over the phone!

Lisa: Hummm, what should I do now that I'm home?

Demon: Catch up on the radio; you're a whole week behind! *(Starts singing raucous rock tune.)* Remember those fun tunes?

Lisa *(reaches for radio):* Yeah, maybe that's . . . *(She stops.)* No, I think I'll sing songs from camp. *(She starts one.)*

Demon: No! Not that! I'm so sick of hearing that! Hummm... *(He ponders, then speaks to Lisa):* Hey, remember when you went up front and you got all choked up?

Lisa *(smiling):* Yeah.

Demon: Just think how stupid you looked! That was so uncool!

Lisa: No! I am not ashamed of my feelings for Jesus!

Demon *(to audience):* Oooooh, gag me with a pitchfork! What am I gonna do? Oh! I know . . . . *(Turns to Lisa again.)* Yeah, that was a great decision! You should really be be proud! You did something with your life! You've got your act together now! You're wonderful and you deserve special treatment!

Lisa: No, Jesus did it all. I'm just His servant.

Demon *(to audience):* Oh, I hate it when they start groveling to Him! Hummm. *(To Lisa):* Okay . . . you're more committed to Him, but don't go overboard, keep everything under control! All things in moderation. Settle down. Keep it cool. You don't want to turn other people off, do you? Just keep quiet about it. Don't be obnoxious!

Lisa: Yeah, maybe . . . No! I'm on fire now; I don't want to cool off!

Demon *(to audience):* Ooooh! She recognizes that her faith is a fire! This is bad. This is very bad. I've got to think of something! *(He sits down.)*

Lisa: I know, I'll pray for a while.

Demon: What? Oh, no! Not that! Anything but THAT! *(He leaps up and begins to run around frantically.)* WAIT! Uh, TV! Yeah. You're *way* behind on your TV shows! What's been happening on "Generally Hostile" or "The Edge of Our Lives?"

Lisa: TV? Hummm. I haven't watched for a while . . . . Naw, I'll pray instead.

Demon: Wait! There are other shows! Look at the *TV Guide.* *(He riffles through it.)* There's a special on this afternoon; "The Brady Bunch Meets My Three Sons and Bore Each Other to Death!" *(Lisa begins to get on her knees.)* Oh, no! Not on your knees! *(His buzzer goes off again.)* It's the main office again! *(To Lisa):* Ummm . . . hey! Your new *Glamour* magazine is here. Uhhh . . . why don't you call to find out what Karen is doing? *(To audience):* I hate it when I have to resort to doing good things to get their minds off—oh, you know who! *(To Lisa):* Hey! Why don't you send Phil a letter? You and he got to be such good friends last week—you don't want him to slip away, do you? Maybe you should call your Aunt Marge . . . she gets so lonely! *(Lisa just continues to pray. In desperation, Demon says):* Another day would be better!

Lisa *(looks up):* Hummm, maybe another day *would* be better.

Demon *(jumping up and down in excitement):* Yes, Yes, Yes!! You've had an exhausting week . . . .

Lisa: After all, it *has* been an *exhausting* week.

Demon: You are so close to God now, it's not as if you even need to pray . . . .

Lisa: It's not like I need to pray . . . I'm already so close to God. . . .

Demon: And the excitement you feel now will last you for a *long* time!

Lisa: And I'm sure what I'm feeling now will stay with me. I've got a full tank; I'll just put my faith on cruise control!

Demon *(happily surprised):* Yeah, that's it! Cruise control! *(He giggles.)* Don't worry about it! You can pray anytime! Those sermons'll last you 'till next year!

Lisa *(gets up):* Yeah, I can pray tomorrow. I'm sure I can hear that little voice inside of me telling me it's okay!

Demon *(wickedly):* And those little voices never lie! HAHAHA-HAHAHA! *(Lisa exits.)* Cruise control! That's a good one, I've got to remember that one! There's no such thing as cruise control! If you don't get daily refills, you come to a stop! HAHAHAHA! *(He begins to exit, but turns to audience.)* My favorite strategy! Look back on yesterday, look forward to tomorrow—just keep 'em away from today! *(His buzzer goes off again and he picks up the receiver.)* Boss? Relax! She's harmless! Another day, another victory! *(He hangs up and whistles his way offstage.)*

Curtain

Alice In I-Wonderland

Characters

Alice, high-school senior, confused, easily swayed
March Hare, impatient, brisk, yuppie type
Mad Hatter, shallow and superficial rhymester
Cheshire Cat, party animal, hippy or surfer dude
King, self-important, pompous
Caterpillar, calm but intense voice of reason
Mom, basic mom

Props/Costumes

March Hare, bunny ears and a large timepiece
Mad Hatter, a stack of hats that match his characters: gang-
    ster stetson, blue tennis visor, wild wig, nerd glasses, halo
Cheshire Cat, long, blonde hair and cat nose
King, crown
Caterpillar, skinhead or bald wig

Performance Tips

Because none of the dream characters are ever on stage
together, all can be played by one, versatile actor(ess), if
desired.

A harp or autoharp glissando may be used as a sound effect
to indicate the beginning and ending of the dream.

Scene: Alice's living room, which will also serve as the location
    for her dream.

Alice *(pacing in frustration):*   Life! It's so confusing! So many
    decisions to make! Should I wear pants or a skirt? Go casual
    or dressy? Socks or hose? Which socks? Which shoes?
    Maybe socks over top of shoes? Ooooh, those used to be
    the *big* decisions in my life. Now it's really getting complicat-
    ed! Now everyone's on me to make a decision about what I
    wanna do with my life. Like . . . I'm so sure I'm ready for
    that! My parents wanna know if I'm going to college in
    another town so they can rent my room out! My boyfriend
    wants to know if I'm sticking around town so he can get a
    second job to pay for our dates, which he won't have time

for since he will have a second job! My guidance counselor keeps shoving college catalogs at me and saying, "Get a life, kid!" Can't I just go to high school for four more years and get another diploma? Just when I got my locker combination memorized! Oh, I wonder what to do? *(She sits.)* I wonder . . . I wonder . . . I wonder . . . *(fading)* . . . I wonder. . . . *(She falls asleep with her head in her hands.)*

March Hare *(enters swiftly and desperately frantic):* Oh, I've got to hurry! So little time! So much to be done! *(He paces wide circles around Alice.)*

Alice *(waking up):* What?! Where am I? Who are you?

March Hare *(stops long enough to talk):* To answer those questions in order: First, I said I've got a great deal to do! Secondly, *you* are in "I-Wonderland."

Alice: I-Wonderland?

March Hare: Certainly! You entered it by being indecisive and by wondering what to do! Thirdly, I am the March Hare.

Alice: But this is April!

March Hare: April? Oh, drat! I knew this watch was slow. Well, nonetheless, I'm out of time.

Alice: Out of time for what?

March Hare: Out of time to meet my deadline.

Alice: What deadline?

March Hare: My, aren't we inquisitive? The deadline is this: I've got to get rich before I'm late!

Alice: Late for what?

March Hare: Late as in, "The late March Hare." I simply must get wealthy before I'm dead!

Alice: Oh! That really is a *dead*line! But why do you have to get rich?

March Hare: Why?! Why indeed?! That's what it's all about, Miss. You've got to have money in order to buy the finest things in life—Jaguars and jacuzzis, spiral staircases, and summer beach homes. Without these things, where is the enjoyment in life?

Alice: Well, you don't seem to be enjoying yourself now! You're in too much of a hurry!

March Hare: I've *got* to hurry or I'll be late! I told you that! Interest never sleeps! There are deals to be made! But never mind me . . . let's talk about *you*. This is what you need to do with your future; join my quest! Go for the wealth! Life is so short!

Alice: Hmmmm, maybe so, if I could get used to hurrying!

March Hare: Well, gotta go now! Let me know what you decide . . . . Send me a postcard! *(He starts to exit.)*

Alice: Okay. Bye!

March Hare *(just before he's out of sight):* Oh, be sure to send it hare mail! *(He exits.)*

Alice: Hmmm . . . well, having nice things does sound fun, but it seems like you're always chasing something. Well, I would do it only until I was rich enough. Wait, come to think of it, I never heard of anyone who thought he was rich enough. Oh, I wonder what to do?!

Mad Hatter *(enters with a stack of hats, singing some lilting, carefree tune.)*

Alice: What's with all the hats?

Mad Hatter: Me.

Alice: You?

Mad Hatter: Yes. *(In a singsong rhyme):* I'm with the hats. Or, they are with me. You see, they are all *my* property.

Alice: Just who *are* you?

Mad Hatter: Just who I am is really no matter. But since you must know, I am the Mad Hatter.

Alice: That would explain all the hats. But why do you keep rhyming?

Mad Hatter: 'Cause when you rhyme all the time, people think it's sublime!

Alice: Are you an entertainer?

Mad Hatter: An entertainer? You could say that. In every crowd, I wear a new hat! When I'm with hoodlums, cut-throats, and thugs, then I become this ugly mug. *(Demonstrates gangster look and dons stetson.)* The country clubs all love me too, as long as I wear my preppy blue! *(Dons blue tennis visor.)* This is for when I'm with druggies and freaks *(he dons wild wig)*, and I even fit in with all kinds of geeks. *(Dons nerd glasses.)* I blend in with the Christians I know, by donning this face and righteous halo! *(Assumes a pious expression with halo.)*

Alice: I feel like I'm in a Dr. Seuss book! *(Pause.)* Well, what kind of person are you really? I mean, what's the sense of all this pretending?

Mad Hatter: It's true that I always have to pretend, but one thing's for sure; I've got lots of friends! When you've got friends, you always have fun—you can be liked by every-one!

Alice: Well, I am definitely into friends—but how can you please everyone? I mean, what about your own ideas? What about convictions of right or wrong?

Mad Hatter: You can't have convictions that will not sway, for that would chase some friends away. Pleasing the crowd is the only sport; fit in with all 'cause life is so short! *(He prances off, singing.)*

Alice: I'm really confused; things are getting worse! I crave popularity, but I can't talk in verse! *(Look of confusion.)* Maybe riches are worth seeking, maybe popularity is. . . I just wonder . . .

Cheshire Cat *(comes shuffling on, grinning):* Yo, excellent babe with the muddled brain!

Alice: Huh? What are you grinning about?

Cheshire Cat: Hey, like the grin is in! Since yer laid up with a nastacious case of major mind-fry over what to do, I, the cat from Cheshire, am here to help you scope it all out.

Alice: That's all I need; more advice! Those other two characters. . . .

Cheshire Cat: Hey, shake off those two geekazoids with their bogus ideas. They're messin' with yer mind, babe. That's way too much headwork.

Alice: Well, what do *you* think I oughta do?

Cheshire Cat: It's way simple! Just chill about yer future and live for right now! Whatever makes you smile this moment, zone in on it!

Alice: Well, that could apply to a lot of things. If I did everything I felt like at the moment, I could get into a lot of trouble.

Cheshire Cat: See, there's more dud-esque thinking. You gotta go with what's hoppin', happenin', killin', ragin' now, and let the future take care of itself. C'mon, get a clue! Kick back! Smoke what you must, swallow what you must, do what you must—live for the grin. Take it from the Cheshire cat—life is too short!

Alice: There's that phrase again!

Cheshire Cat: Hey babe . . . I'm way stoked on it, but I gotta tear . . . I'm ghost! *(He exits.)*

Alice: Is this supposed to be helping me? Every time I think I've got life figured out, something new comes along. This cat made sense—sort of. It's sure easier to live *his* way. What was his name?

King *(enters pompously in time to answer her question, loudly):*

Announcing his majesty, the king!

Alice: His majesty?

King: That is correct.

Alice: Who's he?

King: Whatever do you mean?

Alice: You said *"His* majesty." I wanna know who *he* is.

King: Me!

Alice: Then why don't you say "My majesty," since it's you? And besides, what are you the king of?

King: Young lady, this is a completely inappropriate way to address majesty.

Alice: Well, before I can be impressed, I need to know what you're king of. King of comedy? King of swing? King of the hill?

King: I am his majesty, the king. That's all with which you need concern yourself.

Alice: Well, how did you get to be king?

King *(dramatically):* By devoting my life to building a good name, achieving fame and a reputation for greatness. Now crowds everywhere know me, revere me, respect me, and honor me with the title of "king."

Alice: So you're not actually king of anything, are you?

King *(pauses in thoughtfulness):* Well, the important thing is, I *am* king. I'm quite famous, you know.

Alice *(sighs):* All right, lemme predict the ending here. You're going to recommend that I devote my life to doing the same —seeking fame and getting a name for myself.

King: Aaaah, there's nothing that compares to the thrill of knowing that thousands and thousands of ordinary people know you by name. Get in the spotlight, shake the right hands, kiss up to the right persons, until you feel the thrill of fame and power . . . because after all . . . .

Both: Life is too short!

Alice: Right, I've heard that before!

King: Well, my work here is done. *(Hollers):* His majesty, the king, is now exciting! *(He exits.)*

Alice: Thanks for the warning! *(To herself):* Oh, this is just ducky! If I was thoroughly confused before, I'm extremely confused now. What to do?! Get rich? Get lots of friends? Get thrills? Get famous? What do I wanna get?

(During this speech, Caterpillar enters slowly behind Alice. When s/he speaks, she whirls around in surprise.)

Caterpillar: Or, perhaps the question is, what do you wanna give?

Alice: What?! Oh, please, I've got enough to consider. Don't crowd my brain.

Caterpillar: I would like to clear your brain.

Alice: Hey, just what are you—a slug?

Caterpillar *(with great dignity):* I am a caterpillar! But you're right about one thing; you've got too many forces pulling on you, telling you to how to live. You need only *one* thing on your mind. *(Pause.)*

Alice: Well, what is it?

Caterpillar: Live to give.

Alice: Live to give? Oh, *that* sounds like a blast!

Caterpillar: That's the mystery of it all. You won't truly enjoy life unless you're giving—helping others. Do you enjoy being confused?

Alice: What do you think?! Of course not!

Caterpillar: Then why not live to help others come out of confusion?

Alice: Hey, why am I listening to you anyway? You're just a caterpillar.

Caterpillar: Yes, but someday, I'll be a butterfly. Because now, instead of collecting, I give away. Instead of trying to compete with everyone, I guide them along.

Alice: But . . . life is so short!

Caterpillar: Yes, life is short, and then you die, only to face the One who gave it all away. There is no greater joy . . . no greater joy . . . no greater joy . . . *(he fades away).*

Alice *(wanders back to her chair, sits, and puts her head in her hands):* No greater joy? Oh, I don't know. I just wonder . . . wonder . . . .

Mom *(enters and begins to shake Alice):* Alice, Alice, wake up! There's too much to do for you to be napping! Too many decisions to make!

Alice: What?! Oh, Mom! I had the weirdest dream! There was this rabbit in a hurry, and a guy with a bunch of hats who rhymed, and a cat, and a king and a caterpillar. And they all gave me advice. It was so totally wild! But I think I know what I wanna do now. *(She stands up.)* I wanna be a butterfly!

Mom *(gives Alice a weird look):* C'mon Alice, it was just a dream. *(She begins to guide her offstage.)*

Alice: You mean it all meant nothing?

Mom: Of course, dear. *(Pause.)* Well, all except what the caterpillar said. *(They exit, with Alice giving the audience a perplexed look.)*

Curtain

An Everyday Thing

Characters
Director (Jesus)
Roberta Juliard, prideful, overly dramatic actress
Mary Wells, aspiring actress, shy, unsure
Perry, stage manager

Setting
The stage of a playhouse.

Props/Costumes
Two scripts

A director's chair adds a nice touch. Having the director seated with his back to the audience creates an air of mystery about his identity.

The other characters need no special costumes or treatment.

Scene: *As the curtain opens, the director is already seated near the front of the stage with his back to the audience. Perry escorts the two girls toward him.*

Perry: Sir, here are two more actresses to audition for the play, "An Everyday Thing." This is Roberta Juliard . . . .

Roberta *(moves forward and interrupts):* A very good day to you, sir. May the sun shine on your face, may the wind be at your back and may time itself grace your feet with the path of lessor resistance.

Perry: And this is Mary Wells.

Mary *(shyly):* Hello, sir.

Director: Hello, both of you. Perry, would you please hand them each a script?

Perry: Yes sir. *(Hands a script to both, then exits.)*

Director: This is a play about happiness. Not ordinary happiness—like a bubble that can burst, but happiness that lasts. Happiness that flows from the heart and soul. Anyone can have it, but very few attain it. The section I want you to read is the central point of this play called "An Everyday Thing." You will find it highlighted on page ten. Roberta, please begin.

(Roberta and Mary each find the page, then Roberta steps forward, flips back her hair, and begins.)

Roberta: Happiness? I'll tell you what happiness is. The one who is happy is the one who cries for the wrong in the world. *(Looks up from the paper to add her own line):* Or at least for the wrong done to them! *(Returns to the script):* People who are happy are the gentle ones. Not those who are weak, but gentle—like a bridled stallion. *(Stops for a second, looks puzzled, then continues.)* And the happy ones are those who hunger for what is right *(looks puzzled)*. Happy are they who are flavored with compassion *(looks questioningly at the director and comments):* This script could use a little work. It isn't describing real happiness—this is unbelievable. How can I convey something so phony, so unreal?

Director: The script is true, and it can be acted. I know, I've done this play. You may need a little help, but that is what a director is for, to help you.

Roberta: Well, I don't believe that anyone could help me with this!

Director *(patiently)*: Oh, I'm sure I can help you.

Roberta *(angrily)*: No! I don't see how it can work and I won't do it! *(She shoves the script into the director's hands and walks out.)*

(The director sadly looks after her then slowly lowers his head. After a few seconds, he lifts his head and looks at Mary.)

Director: Mary, would you please pick up where she left off?

Mary *(clears her throat and speaks nervously without conviction)*: Happy is, uh, the one who can get inside another's skin to see his or her side of life. *(Continues without much feeling, making several mistakes.)* These are the ones who are, uh, free from the mask and feel clean in what they do. *(Slight pause.)* And happy is the one who makes peace between God and man and between man and man. These are, uh, the ones who are wronged for the right, yet even in this they are happy. *(She finishes and looks puzzled.)*

Director: Are you having trouble with this script?

Mary *(nodding her head)*: I'm sorry. I know I made a lot of mistakes. I don't know if I could ever perform this. The wording is easy, but I just don't understand the meaning . . . . Is this true happiness? Have *you* really made this play work? Can it be believable?

Director: Yes, I have. And yes, it is believable. *(Looks at the script in his hands.)* The words were a little different when I performed it, but the meaning was the same. This is how I did it. *(He stands and turns toward the audience.)*
   Blessed are the poor in spirit, for theirs is the kingdom of heaven. Blessed are those who mourn, for they will be comforted. Blessed are the meek, for they will inherit the earth. Blessed are those who

hunger and thirst for righteousness, for they will be shown mercy. Blessed are the pure in heart, for they will see God. Blessed are the peacemakers for they will be called sons of God. And Blessed are those who are persecuted because of righteousness, for theirs is the kingdom of heaven.

Mary *(very excited):* Oh! That was wonderful! Now I understand the lines! I want to learn to deliver the lines like you do, to act like you do. I want to *be* more like you. *(Suddenly sad, looks down):* But why would you choose me for a part in "The Everyday Thing"?

Director: The question is not me choosing you, but whether *you* will allow *me* to direct you.

Mary: Please direct me, please teach me. I have a lot to learn. *(Pause, becomes scared.)* What if I can't do it?

Director: That's why I'm here. I'm the director—with my help you can do anything. Come, follow me and I'll show you.

(They walk off with the director pointing to the script and talking silently.)

Curtain

Bargoumbia

Characters
Narrator
Great Doctor, good, kind, Christ-like
Intern #1, sappy and selfish, played melodramatically
Intern #2, same as #1
Sickie #1, diseased and dying
Sickie #2, same as #1
Sickie extras, as many as you wish

Setting
The jungles of Bargoumbia. All that is necessary, beyond the audience's imagination, are two chairs with a table between them, designating the intern's hut. Go as far as you wish with scenery.

Props/Costumes
A huge, thick book to serve as the medical encyclopedia
Pencils, paper
Three smocks (White dress shirts worn backwards do nicely.)
One pith helmet

Performance Tips

Practice the timing as the narrator leads into speaking parts by the characters. Too long a pause between the lines will cause the audience to lose the point. This skit is written as an exaggerated melodrama, but if the actors ham it up *too* much, some of the message will be lost.

Narrator: Long ago and far away, there was a land called Bargoumbia. The land where the people of Bargoumbia made their homes was covered with jungle, and in this jungle, there thrived sicknesses and diseases of every sort. There was much suffering and dying among the Bargoumbians, and what life they had was filled with pain and anguish without relief.

One day, a great doctor came to the jungle. He had heard about the great suffering that plagued the Bargoumbians, and he had come to bring healing. He began to mingle among the afflicted, curing them with his medicine, and nursing them to good health. After many days of dwelling among all the sick, he took aside two patients he had brought back to good health and said to them:

Great: I have been among you long enough. I cannot visit all the sick and afflicted in your land, for it is time for me to go.

Narrator: Before the two could express their dismay he continued:

Great: However, before I go, I will teach both of you how to be doctors like me. When I have finished teaching you, you will have all of the medical knowledge you will need, as well as the proper skill and training, so that after I leave, you may heal and take care of your suffering Bargoumbian brothers and sisters.

Narrator: And so he began training the two, instilling in them all of his vast medical knowledge and teaching them all the skills of medical practice. At times, the interns were . . . well . . . a little dense.

Great: Now then, let's review. As we've learned, what is the present death rate of Bargoumbia?

Intern #1: Uh . . . one per person?

32

Great: Uh . . . yeah. We'll come back to that one. Let's move on to inflammations. First, what is tonsillitis?

Intern #2 *(waves hand vigorously, answers proudly):* Inflammation of the elbow! *(#1 nudges him, points to throat.)* Oh! Tonsils! Tonsillitis is inflammation of the tonsils!

Great: Very good! Now identify appendicitis. (#1 enthusiastically volunteers) Okay, go ahead.

Intern #1: Inflammation of the . . . *(he almost forgets)* . . . Oh! Appendix!

Great: Excellent! Now, what is . . . arthritis? *(The two look at each other in puzzlement, then #2 gets inspired.)*

Intern #2: Inflammation of Arthur!

Narrator: Fortunately, the great doctor had plenty of patience—uh . . . no pun intended. Finally, after many months of personal training, the great doctor was confident that his two interns knew all that they needed to know and could carry on as full-fledged physicians. The great doctor was ready to leave the jungle, but before he did, he said to his two trainees:

Great: You now have the proper knowledge to heal all the sick, diseased, and crippled in your land. Do it. I will leave this medical encyclopedia in which you will find answers to any questions you may have. Now I will leave, but someday I will come back to Bargoumbia to see what you have accomplished. Toodle-loo! *(He exits.)*

Narrator: And he was gone. Although the great doctor had told them what to do, the new doctors could not decide where or how to begin.

Intern #1: Whatever shall we do now?

Narrator: . . . the first one asked.

Intern #1: Shall we plunge right into the task before us?

Intern #2: Oh my, no! We're not ready for that!

Narrator: . . . the second one swiftly replied.

Intern #2: We need to prepare ourselves more fully. Let us study the medical book some more and examine all the healing processes first!

Narrator: The first one pondered a moment, then responded:

Intern #1: Yes! We will build one another up in knowledge! A capital idea!

(From here until the Great Doctor returns, sick and feeble Bargoumbians will hobble, crawl, and carry one another on stage. Appointed ones will crawl towards the intern when he leaves the hut, and others will crawl towards the door of the hut. You may have as many of these extra sickies as you wish, and you may divide up the sickies' lines among them.)

Narrator: And so, in the middle of the jungle, amidst the sick, the diseased, and the dying, the two Bargoumbian doctors, with *all* their knowledge of healing, sat right where they were—and studied the medical encyclopedia. They examined it with a fine-toothed comb, and dwelt on each point of instruction. From time to time, violent arguments would break out between them over one point or another. They did not argue over whether or not a certain disease *could* be cured, or *should* be cured, only on *how* it would be cured. They became so engrossed in their study that months and months passed by without the two doctors ever healing one, single, sick Bargoumbian. The only times they left the hut to go out among the sick were times of dire emergency.

Intern #1: Oh no!!

Intern #2: What? What is it, oh fellow doctor?! What is disturbing you?

Intern #1: Oh! How dreadful! My pencil point snapped and the pencil sharpener is out in . . . the jungle!

Intern #2: Oh no! Then I guess you'll have to go . . . out among the sick!

Intern #1 *(rising triumphantly):* Yes, but it must be done for the sake of our continued study! *(He exits.)*

Intern #2: Remember—avoid the diseased! We've got to stay strong!

Narrator: Whenever either doctor had to step out into the Bargoumbian jungle, they were careful not to get too close to the sick, "Because," they reasoned, "we can't take the chance of getting sick ourselves—we're the doctors!" Now and then, however, one of the dying would manage to stop a dodging doctor.

(Intern #1 enters from one side and Sickie #1 lunges at his ankles.

Sickie #1: Doctor!

Narrator: . . . they would croak in desperation. . .

Sickie #1: Please help us; you've got the knowledge and the power. We're dying!

Narrator: In which case the doctor would nervously reply . . .

Intern #1 Uh, sorry, we don't make house calls. We're still learning, y'know!

Narrator: And then he would run back to the place of research and resume medical study.
 The months turned into years and the two doctors became more and more wrapped up in their training. Remembering the Great Doctor's promise that he would return to see what they'd done, the two decided that they would *really* impress him when he came back. They began writing articles on various points of medical practice, as well as dissertations, theses, and practice manuals. These, they shared with one another and their knowledge of the medical profession became great.
 One day, one of the diseased came crawling to their hut. Before he could speak, one of the doctors cried:

Intern #2: What are you doing here? This is where we study! You are diseased and dying! Go away so we don't become sickly like you!

Narrator: But the diseased Bargoumbian persisted desperately.

Sickie #2: You are the only ones who can make us well. We're all doomed to die! Won't you help?

Narrator: The doctors paused uncomfortably, then one cleared his throat, and spoke.

Intern #1: You see, we must study our medical book so that we can be more knowledgeable in our practice. We're sorry about the condition you're in, but we're not sure we're ready to help you. Good-bye!

Sickie #2: What good is knowledge if you never use it? *(Sobs.)* *Your* knowledge could save us!

Narrator: But the two doctors ignored the sobs of the sick and afflicted and coldly continued in their pursuit of knowledge. Anticipating the Great Doctor's return they studied, compiling volumes and volumes of points and methods of the how-to's of healing. Years churned slowly on in Bargoumbia and the doctors never left their hut. The people fell prey to jungle diseases, and the diseased died. *(Some of the diseased on stage die dramatically.)* And then one day, the Great Physician returned.

(The Great Doctor enters, looks at the sickly bodies all around and says:)

Great: Sick!? Dying!? Where are my doctors?

Sickie #1 *(points feebly in the direction of the doctors and says without expression):* Over there.

(Great Doctor walks over to interns.)

Intern #1: The Great Doctor! Look! The Great Doctor has returned!

Intern #2: Oh, Doctor! It's so good to see you again!

Intern #1: We've waited so long!

Intern #2: And we've got so much to show you! We have

written books and theses and essays and manuals on everything from berylliosis to pellagra to the sniffles!

Intern #2: Whaddya think? Huh? Whaddya think? Pretty impressive, huh?

(The Great Doctor is quiet for a second, then rips their medical smocks off of them. They are shocked.)

Intern #1: Hey, I thought we were doctors?!

Great *(in growing anger):* I healed you and gave you the power to heal others. I depended on you! But you have failed me. How many have died while you isolated yourselves? Now, because you never put your knowledge into practice, it will all be taken from you and you will lose your own lives as well! Go!! *(He points offstage and the two walk miserably away. The Great Doctor begins ministering to each of the sickies while one of the sickies stands up and quotes the Great Commission.)*

Sickie: "Then Jesus came to his disciples and said, 'All authority in heaven and on earth as been given to me. Therefore go and make disciples of all nations, baptizing them in the name of the Father and of the Son and of the Holy Spirit, and teaching them to obey everything I have commanded you. And surely I am with you always, to the very end of the age.'"

Curtain

The Case of the Missing Peace

Characters

Ned Stone, fifteen-year-old detective, cool, calm, not always smart, talks out of the side of his mouth
Mable Bertrim, middle-aged woman, cautious, desperate
Chuck Scott, middle-aged man, easily lead, not too smart

Setting

Cluttered, run-down office of a 1940's-style private eye

Props/Costumes

Ned, 40's-style suit, wide tie loosened at the neck; a trench coat and fedora hanging on a coat rack would be a nice touch
Mable, 40's-style dress, summer hat, and gloves
Chuck, pleated slacks, white shirt, suspenders
Door with "Ned Stone, Private Eye" printed on the "glass," visible from inside the office
Cluttered desk
At least two chairs
Telephone
Business cards

Ned (*sitting at his desk, which is at an angle to stage front, almost facing the audience*): My name is Stone; Ned Stone—the fifteen-year-old private eye. It's a mid-August day—not cool, never is in these kind of stories. It is so sticky hot, in fact, that a gnat landed on my desk a while ago and his feet stuck to the surface. That made him an easy grab, so I fed him to my iguana, Ned Junior. A gnat ain't much of a meal, but this ain't much of a day—boring, no cases in sight. Long time since I had a case. Seems like the last time I had a case, I had to ride a dinosaur to the scene of the crime. Old joke, I know—I told you it's a slow day.

(*He gets up and walks around to the front of the desk.*)
A detective needs mysteries, questions to find answers for. The only questions around here are; why do birds fly south in the winter—why don't they just fly indoors? Who invented soap-on-a-rope, and does anybody really use it?

(Pauses and suddenly realizes): I guess the new question is, why am I asking you?

(There is a knock on the door and it opens. Mable sticks in her head and looks around suspiciously.)

Mable *(coming a little way into the office):* Is this the office of Ned Stone?

Ned *(calmly):* Whose name is on the door, Dollface?

Mable *(turns around and strains to read Stone's name backwards on the closed door):* Uh, e... nots... den... eye... etavirp....

Ned: On the other side of the glass, that spells,"Ned Stone, Private Eye." Answer your question?

Mable: Why, yes. *(Pauses to collect her thoughts.)* I'm here because I have a problem.

Ned: People who come to see me usually do. Take a seat. *(Gestures to chair beside desk.)*

Mable *(sitting):* I could really use your help.

Ned *(calm, cool):* That's why I'm here. That's my business. That's what I'm all about; I'm Ned Stone, detective.

Mable *(notices the iguana behind Ned's desk and screams):* EEEEIII! There's a—there's a giant lizard on your floor!

Ned: Don't panic, doll. *(Looks behind desk):* It's just Ned Junior; he's always getting lost.

Mable *(horrified):* Your *son*?!

Ned: No, my iguana. Would you like to pet him?

Mable: No. Thank you very much. *(Studies Ned.)* May I ask just exactly how old you are?

Ned *(quickly, a little irritated):* Let me ask you a question, Pudding; just exactly how old are the pyramids?

Mable *(puts a finger to her mouth, thinking):* Let's see... I don't think I know for sure.

Ned: Well alright then, sometimes you just can't be too sure, can you? What's your story?

Mable *(looks at him with a puzzled expression which then changes to worry):* Well, yesterday as I was coming home from work, I—

Ned *(interrupts):* Where do you work?

Mable: At the shoe tongue store on Main Street.

Ned: A shoe *tongue* store? What about the shoes?

Mable: We don't sell those.

Ned: You sell shoe tongues without the shoes?

Mable: That's right. Here's my card. *(She takes a card out of her purse and hands it to him.)*

Ned *(reads with a questioning look):* "We are tongues." *(Looks at the audience as if to say, "Do you believe this?" then back at Mable. Says slowly):* I see. Who'd need to buy a shoe tongue without the rest of the shoe?

Mable: You'd be surprised.

Ned: I guess I would. Go on with your story.

Mable: Well, I was driving home from work and—

Ned *(interrupts again):* What kind of car do you have?

Mable *(frustrated):* Are you going to listen to my story or not?

Ned: Listen, Dollhair, let's get one thing straight; to solve any case, I have to get the facts. Now if you're not willing to give all the facts, then I'll just leave right now. *(Gets up and walks over to door.)*

Mable: Mr. Stone?

Ned *(stops and turns toward her):* That's my name.

Mable: This is your office.

Ned *(coughs nervously):* I knew that. Just seeing if you did.

Mable: Right. Okay, here are the facts.

Ned *(sits on his desk):* Spill your guts, Lambchop.

Mable: I was coming home from work and all of the sudden I felt an urge to turn down Broadway and go to a little tie-clip store that I've always wanted to go to. You see, my husband wears ties—

Ned *(stands, suddenly very serious):* That's strange. Call it coincidence or call me at home, but a lot of other people around here are wearing ties, too! *(Pauses to think, sits back down on the desk and then says seriously):* Tell me more.

Mable: Well, I had just gotten out of my car when a street evangelist came up to me and asked if I had peace—

Ned *(excitedly):* What would he want with a gun?

Mable: A gun?

Ned *(quickly, with a gradual increase in intensity):* Piece—a gun; a piece is another name for a gun—that's detective talk. I shudder to think what an evangelist would want with a gun. . . . *(Pauses to think.)* Those poor people who don't come down the aisle when he calls! *(Jumps up):* We've got to find him—let's go! We've got to stop him! *(Starts to pull her out of her chair.)* Some of those people don't even need to come forward!

Mable: No, no! That's not what he meant!

Ned *(embarrassed, tries to regain his composure):* Sure, I knew that. I was just testing your story. *(Walks back to his seat.)*

Mable: Are you on any medication or anything?

Ned: "On" medication? *(Slight pause.)* Well, I do have some aspirin in my back pocket; do you need some?

Mable: That will depend on how long this takes! *Anyway,* the evangelist asked if I had peace and I told him yes. But then I got to thinking about it, and I realized that *(slight pause, looks down,)* I really don't.

Ned: So you don't have a gun. Why do you need me?

Mable *(pleading):* Ned, I need you to find peace for me!

Ned: Piece? Piece of what? A piece of the action, a piece of old fruitcake, what?

Mable: Peace of heart!

Ned: Doll, you don't need me, you need a doctor. *(He pulls out a card.)* Here's a fifteen-year-old surgeon by the name of Bowser.

Mable: No, Mr. Stone! Not my *physical* heart! I just don't seem to have peace in my soul anymore.

Ned: Well, no wonder—all you sell are shoe tongues. Maybe you should try selling the rest of the shoe—especially the sole! That would probably make a lot of people happy.

Mable *(desperate):* No, no! I'm talking about my *spiritual* soul!

Ned: Oh. *(Realization hits.)* Oh! Now I understand! *(Thinks for a minute.)* Looks like you came to the wrong place. But, people usually do look in the wrong places when it comes to spiritual matters.

Mable: What do you mean?

Ned: Just this, Cupcake. People try all kinds of roads to peace; money, possessions, friends, family, dating services, The Rose Ann Barr show. . . but none of these things ever work. The laughs stay with you only until the last credit. That's because the credit goes to man. What you need is more than man— you need the *ultimate* detective. *(Slight pause.)* But His price is very high.

Mable: Money is no object.

Ned *(thoughtfully):* No, money usually *is* the object—but finding peace with this detective requires more than money, Sweet pea.

Mable: What else could it take?

Ned: Everything you've got. You'll have to hand your whole life over.

Mable *(worried):* That's a very high price, Ned.

Ned: You've got that right, Babe. But, after all, He paid the ultimate price for peace, so He expects a lot from you.

Mable: Who is this guy?

Ned *(reaches into his pocket):* Here's His card. *(Hands it to Mable.)*

Mable *(reading):* Jesus Christ?! Oh! *(Looks at Ned, then back at card.)* His address is, "In This Very Room." Toll-free number, "1-800-P-R-A-Y-E-R-S. *(Looks questioningly at Ned.)*

Ned: That's right, you don't even need a phone. He's right next to you.

Mable *(startled, looks around):* Where?

Ned: He is *spiritually* right next to you.

Mable *(getting up):* Wow! Thank you so much, Ned! You may be young, but you're good!

Ned: Doll, truth is truth at any age. *(Stands up and hands her another card.)* And here's the number of the church at the end of the block. *(Says with a smile):* Now get out of here before I get such a big head that my hat won't fit!

Mable *(very happy):* Oh, thank you, thank you! *(She leaves, looking at the cards.)*

Ned *(addressing the audience while he returns to sit on his* *desk):* Another day, another story; that's why I'm here, that's my job. You see, in every case there's a beginning and an end. This case was no different—

Chuck *(Comes rushing into the office):* Mr. Stone! Mr. Stone!

Ned: The name's Stone, Ned Stone, fifteen-year-old private eye.

Chuck *(nervous and excited):* My name is Chuck Scott, Mr. Stone, and my tongues are missing!

Ned: I see. Well, maybe the cat got 'em?

Chuck: Nah. I think my dog got 'em; he was chewing on my sneakers. Can you help me? I hate wearing sneakers with no tongues!

Ned *(looking at audience):* Well, whaddaya know? The Doll-face was right! *(Looks back to Chuck):* Missing tongues are no problem for Ned Stone. *(Reaches into his pocket for Mable's card.)* This is the place you need, my friend. *(Winks at the audience as he hands Chuck the card.)*

Chuck: Wow! You're really something! Thanks, Mr. Stone! You're amazing!

Ned *(trying to be modest):* You bet! Now, get outta here before I get as stuck-up as the gnat on my desk!

(Chuck leaves and Ned sits on his desk facing the audience.)

Ned: I guess it's not such a slow day after all; I've had all the action I can take on a hot day like this. By the way, how 'bout you? Do you need peace in your life? Then follow the hottest tip since time started ticking; find Jesus Christ. *(Pauses, then looks quickly around on the floor.)* Say, any-body seen my iguana?

Curtain

The Decision Zone

Characters
Desert Guy, dusty, dirty, almost dead from lack of water
Rod Swerling, the smooth-talking voice of "The Decision
Zone." Well-dressed, very serious

Setting
A desert. A pump is centerstage.

Props/Costumes
Sand
Pump
Canteen
Box, note, jar of water
Ragged, torn, dusty clothes for Desert Guy
Dark suit with narrow lapels for Rod
Prerecorded sound of running water
Prerecorded theme from "The Twilight Zone" (optional)
Prerecorded background music (optional)

Performance Tips
The desert guy needs to take his time and be dramatic when
making his decision. Dramatic background music may be
helpful.

Scene: *A desert, with a water pump centerstage. The desert guy
staggers in from either side. He does not see the pump. He has a
canteen strapped over his ragged clothes and he is at the point
of death. Theme from "The Twilight Zone" comes up and fades
as the guy starts to speak.*

Desert Guy: Water! I need water! *(He takes a few more stag-
gering steps, then falls slowly to the ground. He freezes while
Rod speaks.)*

Rod *(walks between pump and desert guy)*: Decisions, decisions; life is full of them. The difficulty in making decisions

comes from caring about the outcome. Sometimes, one's very life may hang in the balance. *(Points to the desert guy.)* He's lost in the desert, and he's about to be faced with a decision. Could it be that he is trapped in a seemingly endless sea of sand, looking for water that might never be there? Or—if he finds water, what will it cost him? The answer to these questions can only be answered in the scorching desert of. . . The Decision Zone. *(Rod exits as dramatic music builds in the background).*

Guy *(crawls toward the pump in anguish. He stops and opens his canteen, but it is full of sand, which he pours slowly out onto the ground. He starts to crawl again. As the music builds to a climax, he bumps his head into the pump and in amazement and shock, coughs up dust. [Lifts hand as if to cover mouth, but hand contains sand, which he "coughs" away.] Quickly he tries to get water out of the pump, but fails. He falls forward with a cry of anguish, totally drained of energy. After a few seconds, he lifts his head and sees a box with a note on the top. Slowly lifting himself onto his knees, he picks up the letter and reads):*

Voice: Greetings traveler! I am the keeper of this pump. I hope you are having a pleasant journey. *(Guy reacts with an exasperated exhale.)* You may be a little thirsty, or wish to refill your water containers. If you would like some fresh water, you must first saturate the leather gasket inside this pump by pouring water into the top.

Guy *(screams in anger and frustration):* I don't have any water!! *(He starts to read again.)*

Voice: Yes, you do. Inside the box is a jar of water for use in priming the pump. But you *must* pour it *all* into the pump! If you drink any of the water in the bottle, you will not have enough left to prime the pump, you will not get any fresh, cool water, and you will not be able to leave water for the next traveler to use to prime the pump. However, if you use all the water in the bottle to prime the pump, you will be rewarded with an unlimited supply of sweet water. Please be sure to refill the jar for the next traveler.

Guy: *(throws down the note, rips open the box and pulls out the water. Excitedly, he starts to drink, stops, frowns, looks at* *the letter, at the water, at the letter, at the water, at the pump and nervously puts the water and the letter down.)*

Unlimited sweet water, huh? What if it's a lie? What if it's somebody's idea of a cruel joke? Then I won't have any water. *(Pause.)* Still, this jar isn't enough to get me very far. *(Pause.)* But it's all I've got. *(Pause.)* Sweet, cool water! *(He picks up the jar and looks at it, then the pump. He touches his fingers to the side of the glass, wetting them and touches his lips.)*

Water! Water! *(Looks at the water and pump with greater and greater intensity, grabs his canteen and looks at the desert past the pump.*

I don't know how far I may still have to go. . . . *(He looks back at the jar. After looking again, back and forth from jar to pump, he finally pours the water quickly into the pump with a yell.)*

AHHHHHHHHHH! *(Slowly he works the pump again and again with growing intensity, but no water appears. Finally, he falls onto the ground with a loud cry):* Noooo!

Gradually, the sound of running water is heard, gurgling up from the ground, getting louder and louder. The guy slowly realizes that water is coming. He pulls himself up and stands with his hands outstretched toward the pump.)
Water! *(The water sound stops and the guy falls to his knees, and freezes.)*

Rod *(walks onstage again):* Life or death revolved around words on a piece of paper. If he believed the message, he'd have life for himself, in an abundant supply of water. But in order to get it, he had to give all that he had.
Therein lies an important lesson for us. Sometimes, to get all, we have to give all. This could mean our money, talent, time, even our life. Our desert guy believed the words on the paper and he gave his all. The question for us is, what are we willing to give for what we believe? The answer for each of us remains in . . The Decision Zone.

("Twilight Zone" music comes up as the curtain comes down.)

A Free-Falling Mission

Characters
Grain of Salt #1, depressed, nervous, lost his flavor
Grain of Salt #2, good, willing to work
Male and female voices with a country accent for three lines. Could be tape recorded beforehand, or live, but should be amplified either way.

Setting
Scene 1, the inside of a salt shaker
Scene 2, on top of a large cut of steak

Props/Costumes
White sheets can be draped around the stage
A huge fork, possibly made out of cardboard covered with aluminium foil
A huge steak, possibly a mattress covered with brown cloth or wrapping paper and painted to look like a steak (optional)
Both performers are dressed entirely in white. May be either male or female

Performance Tips
To perform this skit without a pause between scenes, the "steak" can be on stage, hidden by a white-draped backdrop

(which represents the salt shaker). When the salts are "shaken offstage" prop people can move the backdrop to reveal the "steak," just as the salts tumble back onstage. The huge fork can be hung by wires from overhead, swung in from side stage, or lifted over another backdrop to take a swipe at Salt #1. These oversized props are optional and can be "shown" by the actions of Salts 1 and 2, but they really add life to the skit.

Scene #1: *The inside of a salt shaker.*
Salt #1 *(nervous and frustrated):* I've got to get out of this salt shaker!

Salt #2: I'm with you, pal. I'm getting tired of this.

Salt #1: I can't breath in here! It's too crowded and everybody is dressed alike.

Salt #2: Yeah. Even when I close my eyes, I see white. But, you know, there are some of us in here who are old and yellow.

Salt #1: Yeah, I've seen some of 'em. Boy, what a shame.

Salt #2: Maybe we should be glad that we're still white!

Salt #1 *(scared):* Yeah, yeah.

Salt #2: Say, come to think of it, you don't look so good. You look like you've lost some of your spice of life.

Salt #1: I'm just tired of being in here.

Salt #2: Hey, you have to stay ready! Get excited! At any moment, the big hand could come to tip us over, and then we'll escape through those holes up there. *(Points and looks up.)*

Salt #1 *(looking up):* I'd like nothing better.

Salt #2: We *could* still be at the bottom, like we were last month!

Salt #1: Boy! We *really* couldn't breath down there—and I was right next to a big, fat, ugly, yellow piece of rice!

Salt #2 *(shudders):* Ooooooh! What a bummer. *(Gets excited again.)* But here we are at the top! Right on top of the shaker community. What a thrill! This means we could be next!

Salt #1: The last time we got the big shake, I almost made it out, *(gulps)* but I'm glad I didn't.

Salt #2: Why?

Salt #1: Well, *(points up and demonstrates the event)* the big hand came and we were all tipped over, but as I got next to the top, I saw something horrible.

Salt #2: What was it?

Salt #1: The big hand was using our brother salts in a horrible, despicable way! *(He puts his hands on either side of his face and shakes his head.)*

Salt #2: The dog?

Salt #1: Yes!

Salt #2 *(shuddering):* Ohhhhhhhh!

Salt #1: Thousands of our fellow sodiums were being licked up by *(pause, grimace):* a dog's tongue!

Salt #2 *(shakes head sadly):* They didn't even get a chance to spice something.

Salt #1 *(swallows hard):* Yeah! *(Looks around):* Man, what else could go wrong? Everybody looks exactly the same in here, I can't breathe, and we could get licked up by a big, old, wet, slobbery, dog tongue!

Salt #2 *(slightly crying):* When it rains, it pours! *(Encouragingly):* But you've got to cheer up; soon we'll be out doing our jobs—adding flavor!

Salt #1: I'm not sure I want to do that anymore.

Salt #2: Hey, don't say that! That would really make Papa Morton sad. You've got to get pumped about flavoring!

50

You've got to get—iodized!

Salt #1 (*thinking*): Well, maybe you're right. But what if this house is on a low sodium diet?

Salt #2: No way! That's always just big talk!

Salt #1 (*still upset*):   But what if we land on brocolli, or (*shudders*) asparagus?

Salt #2 (*excited*):   What if we land on steak?

Salt #1:   Oh, well, that's different. (*Relaxes a little.*) I wouldn't mind flavoring then; that would be great.

Salt #2: Well, keep that in mind because we just might—

(*Both start to sway and move as if the shaker were moving.*)

Salt #2: Look, it's the big hand! (*Points up.*) It's time!

(*Their voices fade as they tumble offstage*):

Salt #1: This is it! Here comes the shake!

Salt #2 Head for the hoooooles!

(*They both fall and tumble offstage.*)

Scene 2: *A large cut of steak. As the scene opens, both salts fall onto the steak.*
Salt #1 (*standing up*):   Wow! What a fall! (*Rubs neck.*)

Salt #2 (*looking up*):   Yeah, we must have fallen almost a foot! (*Looks at #1*): But hey! We're free! And look! We're on steak! No brocolli, no asparagus!

Salt #1: You're right—it *is* steak! (*Both jump up and down in excitement.*)

Salt #2 (*stops jumping and says with awe*): What a mission!

Salt #1 (*stops jumping, gets serious*):   Mission? What do you mean?

Salt #2: A free-fall spicing mission—and on steak! This is our big chance to do what we were created for!

Salt #1: It's our big chance to get out of here! *(Starts to leave.)*

Salt #2 *(grabs #1 and pulls him back):* Hey! You can't leave! We're *salt!* It's time for us to melt into the steak to give it flavor! This is our job. This is what we've been waiting to do!

Salt #1 *(horrified):* Are you kidding? If we melt, we die! Like, that's it—life is over!

Salt #2: Yeah, but what a way to go, what glory! We add flavor to the steak—or, *(a little angry):* whatever we land on for that matter! I thought you said that if we landed on steak, you would be willing to flavor.

Salt #1 *(whining):* Well. . . well. . . I thought it would be different! I don't want to die. *(Begging):* Let's get out of here— let's go live a little! I've kind of lost the *taste* for this job!

Salt #2 *(disappointed with #1):* I guess you have. *(Pause.)* But I'm not leaving, I can't; I've got to do my job. It's already getting late—good-byyyyyeeeee. . . . *(falls down slowly and happily as if melting—if your "steak" is thick enough, he can disappear behind it).*

Offstage male voice: Hey, Martha, there's one grain of salt on my steak that isn't melting!

Offstage female voice: Oh, Harold, you're so particular!

Male: Maybe so, but it's my steak; I'm gonna knock it off.

(A huge fork swings through the air and knocks Salt #1 off the steak—or, #1 just acts as if he's been knocked off.)

Salt #1 *(gets up and looks around excitedly):* Hey, this is great; I'm free! What a party! *(Suddenly looks up and becomes horrified.)* Oh no! Here comes a huge foot! I'm gonna be trampled, crushed! Oh no! Noooooo. . . . *(voice trails off as he runs offstage.)*

Curtain

Home Worship Kit

Characters
Announcer, an offstage voice speaking in a slick, hard sell, huckster fashion

Man, not too intelligent, but always has a smile

Setting
A bedroom

Props
Bed

Alarm clock

Cassette player

Huge, gaudy sign containing Home Worship Kit address

Large box, decorated to look like an actual commercial product. Audience should be able to read, "Home Worship Kit" on it. The box should be small enough to

be thrown but large enough to hold all the Home
Worship Kit paraphernalia, including:
    Cassette (may be blank, real sound-effects will come
      from offstage)
    Hymnbook
    Prayer book
    Communion Kit
    Meditation Cards
    Offering Plate
    Sermonette File
    Stained-glass spectacles (sunglasses with bits of col
      ored paper glued on the lenses)
Sound effect tape, containing:
    (each segment need last only 5-10 seconds)
    Pipe organ prelude (described as "depressing")
    Choir singing a familiar hymn
    Waterfall of coins tumbling into a metal plate, followed
      by a computerized voice saying, "Thank you!"
    More organ music that reaches a crescendo at climax of
      commercial

Scene: *Bedroom. Man is asleep on bed.*
Announcer *(in glitzy, camp announcer style:)* Are you tired of
waking up ridiculously early on Sunday mornings to attend a
stuffy house of worship and sit on a hard pew? *(An alarm
clock goes off, which man smashes.)* Are you tired of feeling
guilty for sleeping in on that holy morning? *(Man holds head
in anguish.)* Well, suffer no more! Now, from Wrongo, you
can have the Home Worship Kit!

*(Man sits on the edge of bed. Suddenly, a Worship Kit is tossed
to him from off stage, and he adroitly catches it.)*

Announcer: With the Wrongo Home Worship Kit, you can
experience all the elements of a Sunday-morning church
service in the comfort and privacy of your own home, without so much as slipping out of your pajamas. First, set the
proper mood of reverence with a pipe-organ prelude. It is
available on this cassette "Somber Organ Hymns to Knot
Your Brow," played by world renowned church organist
Raymond Dirgely.

*(Man pops cassette into player. Depressing organ music plays
over PA system while man looks exaggeratedly pious.)*

Announcer: Now it's time for *you* to sing. Hear your favorite beloved hymns sung by the 465 voice Mammon Pumpernickel Choir while you follow along in your own personal hymnbook.

(Man sings hideously off-key with a hymn book.)

Announcer: You can sing off-key, muff over the words, or not sing at all. It's your option, because, *no one is listening!* HA!HA!HA!HA! When you've sung all you've wanted, it's time for prayer—but don't worry. No need to overtax your brain thinking of the right words to utter—it's all done for you with the Home Worship Kit.

(At the beginning of this speech, the man on the bed at first looks worried, then relieved as he pulls out the prayer book.)

Announcer: Included in our packet is this booklet "Pious Prayers for All Occasions." Yes, a collection of richly worded prayers written by various saints throughout the ages, complete with Helen Steiner Rice verses, and all articulated in beautiful King James English to impress the deity.

(Man mumbles through a few, showing difficulty in following the text.)

Announcer: Can something as vital as Communion be omitted from your worship experience? Heavens, NO! The Home Worship Kit has it all! With the Wrongo Communion Packet, no more fuss, muss and bother—all the work is done for you.

(Man fumbles through the various elements.)

Announcer: Read over one of the illustrated Lord's Supper Meditation Cards, then partake of the emblems. The unleavened bread is Scripturally pre-cut to an exactly righteous nibble, and the fruit of the vine pre-measured to an exactly pious swallow. Nip, sip, and bow with our Communion packet.

Now it's offering time! You'll love the Wrongo Home Offering Plate. *(Man holds it up to display.)*

Announcer: The smallest widow's mite deposited emits the sound of a huge volume of coinage, with a computerized voice expressing gratitude. *(Pause for coin and computerized "Thank You" sound effect.)* And there's no more wasting your precious time listening to a minister drone on and on with his sermon—all the inspiration you'll need is in our Wrongo Sermonette File. *(Man starts sifting through index card file or Rolodex.)*

Announcer: We have miniature essays on colorful index cards to suit every mood . . . and there will be no more squirming and shuffling, battling feelings of guilt; all Wrongo sermonettes are *guaranteed* to avoid any personal applications or doctrinal dogmatism! Select from such titles as:
"Let's Ponder a Dandelion,"
"Kickball—the Forgotten Sport,"
"The Salamander Can be Your Friend," and more.
(Man is reading through a card he selects, grinning all the while.)

Announcer: Now, a bit more organ mood music, and you're finished! *(Organ music continues to the end.)* You've accomplished your spiritual obligations for the week, and how easy it was! Now, the Wrongo Home Worship Kit can be yours for only $19.95. That's right, $19.95! Plus, if you act now, we'll also send these unique stained-glass spectacles.
(Man hams it up with specs.)

Announcer: Add that cathedral atmosphere to your view of the world. *(Man leans over and lifts up a huge card containing the Home Worship Kit address. This has been face down on the floor throughout the skit.)*
Send $19.95 to:
Home Worship Kit
705 Booth Aid Way
Rockville, MD 01414
Now, worship has never been *more convenient!*

Curtain

Hope for the Body

Characters
Connie Ching, TV reporter, wants the best for God's work
Ear, aloof and haughty
Elbow, gruff, redneck type
Finger, spacey, laid-back, hippy-type
Toenail, Mousey, insecure nerd with low self-esteem

Setting
The Body of Christ , on a TV news documentary. Although the reporter is touring the "body" of Christ, it is necessary to leave this up to the audience's imagination.

Props/Costumes

The body travel vehicle—This can be a chair or platform that Connie sits or stands on, along with a stand to serve as the instrument panel. Body travel may indicated by sound effects and lights if you choose.

Characters would do well to wear costumes that reflect their personalities, such as:

Ear, high-society glasses, clothes stuffed with pillows
Elbow, ball cap or hard hat
Finger, hippy wig and/or glasses
Toenail, nerd glasses and/or hairstyle

Performance Tips

To bring the illusion of high-tech instruments at work, lighting and sound effects can be easily employed. If you have theatrical lighting, flash hot colors while the travel machine is operating. A portion of the ceiling lights can be switched off and on for the same effect. A tape of computer or sci-fi synthesizer sounds playing in the background at the same time would also be optimum.

The four body parts interviewed are distinct characters. You can have a lot of fun with them and make the skit more entertaining by adding exaggerated character voices. If you feel you'd like to make their identities more obvious to the audience, each character could wear a tee-shirt with his or her respective title (or picture) emblazoned on the front.

If you are limited on actors, one person can play all four body parts, provided he or she has the versatility to convey four distinctly different characters. In such an arrangement, the tee-shirts and costumes mentioned would be a great help.

Connie Ching can be played by a male by changing the name to Hugh Drowns, or some other altered name of a recognizable investigative reporter.

Connie Ching: Good evening, ladies and gentlemen and welcome to that incisive but short new show, "Twenty Minutes." I'm Connie Ching. Tonight we will be investigating what's been going on in the Body of Christ. We've sensed much alarm from those on the outside concerned with the apparent ill health of the Body of Christ—the frailty, the sluggishness, the pale appearance. We decided to look into it further . . . and I do mean, "look into." By means of an advanced, state-of-the-art, scientific breakthrough, we're actually able to enter the Body itself and get an inside look at what's been causing the problems. Let's go in. *(She steps onto a platform and presses buttons on the stand. All sorts of high-tech sounds are heard.)* Amazing! *(She steps off.)* In just a few seconds we've made entry. Let's see what we find. It looks as if we're in the upper neck region.

(Ear enters, stuffed with pillows.)

C.C.: Ah, yes . . . here's the ear. Perhaps he knows something. *(She approaches ear.)* And you, I presume, are the ear?

Ear: I heard that!

C.C.: My, I can't help but notice . . . you're awfully swollen, aren't you?

Ear: A little, I suppose, but I think it enhances my looks, don't you?

C.C.: Well, actually. . . .

Ear: Being swollen helps people to notice me more. There I sit on the side of the head, looking majestic, picking up all sound waves . . . an amazing task, if I do say so myself! And what an elegant sight I am, from the upper folds all the way down to the lobe. Why else do people like to nibble on ears?

C.C.: Well, you look rather like a dried apricot to me . . . .

Ear: Without me, where would earrings hang? From the eyelids? Barbers wouldn't know where not to cut! Sunglasses would slide down the face, not to mention the fact that no one could listen to anything.

C.C. *(aside):* I get the feeling that no one's listening now. *(To ear:)* But don't you feel like you're sticking out awfully far from the head?

Ear: Why shouldn't I stick out? Without me, the body would be helpless . . . totally unattractive, unable to function . . . lost . . . sunk!

C.C.: But don't you see that when you're swollen like this, you're sore, and easily irritated? And the rest of the body has to work extra hard to make sure nothing brushes against you.

Ear: Sounds right to me! Why shouldn't they protect me? Where would they be without me?

C.C.: But when you're so swollen, you don't hear as well as you should.

Ear: Fine, thank you. And you?

C.C.: I rest my case.

Ear: Well, you go ahead and pick your face . . . I've got some waxing to do *(Exits.)*

C.C.: Well, we've pinpointed one problem. Let's see if there are others. *(She steps on the platform, pushes buttons and again we hear the electronic sounds.)* Ah, the wonders of modern science! *(She steps off.)* I believe we're in the arm region now.

(Elbow very stiffly shuffles in.)

C.C.: Hmmm, who's this? Let's investigate *(She crosses to elbow.)* And who are you?

Elbow *(remains stiff throughout dialogue):* Elbow.

C.C.: Well, you look a little stiff, Elbow.

Elbow: Yup, I suppose.

C.C.: What's the problem?

Elbow: Don't feel like doing nothin'!

C.C.: Why not?

Elbow: I'm afraid of getting overworked. Might get bumped. Might get bruised! The knees and elbows are always taking abuse, so we all got together and agreed not to do nothin'.

C.C.: When did you decide this?

60

Elbow: At a joint meeting.

C.C.: Yes, of course. But don't you realize what you're doing? By refusing to work, you're keeping the rest of the arm inactive . . . the hand, the fingers, not to mention the fact that the rest of the body is overworked trying to make up for your loss. Why . . . you're causing paralysis!

Elbow: Causing it? I can't even say it. But anyhow, I just don't wanna take the chance. It's too much strain to work. I'd rather just sit here and do nothing. *(He falls asleep, then shuffles off in a daze.)*

C.C.: This is getting more pathetic as time goes on! Let's move to another section. *(She steps on platform and mimes pressing buttons on a panel.)* Let's have a look at the end of the arm. It's handy from here. *(More electronic noises.)* Ah, yes, here we are—I can see the palms . . . I can feel the warm breezes! *(She steps off. Finger enters, jerking and spinning and moving spastically like a hyperactive kid.)* Oh, and you are . . . ?

Finger: Finger! Finger, Finger, Finger!

C.C.: What exactly are you doing?

Finger: Me? My own thing, man! I've gotta be me. I've got to express my own personality—have my own identity, you know.

C.C.: I see. Well, what exactly is this accomplishing for the rest of the Body?

Finger: Oh, I don't know. And I don't really care, Dude. Like, they do their thing and I do mine. I'm not into being told what to do. I don't need them.

C.C.: Maybe you don't realize it, but a finger acting by itself can look pretty crazy. It makes the whole body look spastic. When you do as you please, its a bad reflection on all the body parts.

Finger: Now don't go tryin' to lay a guilt trip on me! I know the head of this body—Jesus. Him, I know. I just don't get along with these other parts.

C.C.: But that's just it! You've *got* to think of the others! You, the elbow, the ear . . . . If you'd only realized that when the parts of His body aren't working right, it makes Jesus, the head, look mighty shabby.

Finger: Oh come now, I doubt that it's *that* serious.

C.C.: Oh, but it is!

Finger: Oh? What's He gonna do, die?

C.C.: No. He won't die again. But you will. Jesus has said that if you insist on going your own way long enough, you'll stop getting signals from the head. Check your nerve endings—do you feel anything anymore?

Finger *(feeling himself):* Am I touching myself? Am I making contact? I can't tell! *(To Connie):* Here pinch me . . . poke me! *(Connie complies.)* Go ahead! *(Starting to panic.)* C'mon! Oh no! . . . it can't be . . . no more feelings! *(He exits, shouting fearfully all the way.)*

C.C.: Phew! I thought talking to the finger would be a snap. Wow, this is getting touchy! Are *any* of the components doing their part? Let's go all the way to the foot; I want to get to the bottom of this. *(She does the platform routine.)* Well, this is all the farther we can go. Let's see who we find. *(Toenail enters)* Hello, there!

Toenail: Oh . . . hi.

C.C.: Hey, why so downcast? Aren't you from around here?

Toenail: Toenail's the name. But how I wish I were something else.

C.C.: Something else? But why?

Nail: Why do you think? I'm hard and brittle and ugly. I just stick out of the toes, which are homely enough by themselves. I've gotta get clipped all the time or else I'll punch holes in slippers or get ingrown. No one likes us toenails.

C.C.: Now, what makes you say that?

Nail: Because! They bury us in those big loathsome cloth bags so no one can see us. And they STINK!

C.C.: Are you talking about socks?

Nail: Oh, call them what you wish. A hose by any other name still smells. Why couldn't I be an eye? Always out front looking beautiful . . . long lashes . . . gorgeous colors, giving sight.

C.C.: Now wait a minute! You *protect* the the toes! *You're* the armor that keeps them from getting squashed!

Nail: Really?

C.C.: Sure! With sore toes, the whole body would be unable to walk. Who says you gotta be out in the open to be important?

Nail *(pauses, considering):* Wow! I never thought of myself that way! I *am* important. *I* can make a difference! One thing about toes . . . you can always count on them—as long as I'm protecting them! I've got a new attitude! I'll do my part gladly! *(He stands tall and proud, and flexes.)*

C.C.: That's the spirit! *(Begins to look around.)* Hey, look . . . do you see it? *(If possible, have red lights begin to slowly emerge, with a rumbling sound.)* There's a new glow in the body—you can see the health coming back! *(She begins to rock, as if in a mild tremor.)* And . . . yes! It's beginning to stir! *This* is what happens when each member does it's part; the body of Christ is on the move again! *(Turns to audience):* Well folks, you saw it here! This is Connie Ching reporting live from the Body of Christ for "Twenty Minutes!"

Curtain

How Are You?

Characters
  Julie, a business woman who is a little on edge
  Sandy, an average woman
  Gary, a very troubled man wildly looking for help
  Laura, an average woman

Setting
  Bare stage except for two chairs, stage left

Props/Costumes
  Two chairs

Performance Tips
  The audience will understand the shift from present to past to present more easily if the action takes place on well-defined

portions of the stage. Do not let "past" activities run over into "present" space, and vice versa.

Scene: *Sandy enters from stage left and passes Julie going the other way.*

Sandy: Hello, Julie. How are you?

Julie *(stops):* Do you really want to know?

Sandy *(stops):* Know what?

Julie: What you asked me.

Sandy: When?

Julie: Just now.

Sandy: I said, "hello."

Julie: You asked how I was.

Sandy: How you were when?

Julie: Right now.

Sandy: What?

Julie: You just said, "Hello Julie, how are you?" I want to know if your "How are you?" means "Hey, I'd really like to know how you're feeling," or if it means, "I don't know any other words of greeting and I don't really care."

Sandy: Well, what do you want—a Hallmark? It was just a greeting, okay? What's wrong with you?

Julie: I thought it was just a greeting too, until yesterday. I'd be more careful about asking that question if I were you—that is if you don't really care how the other person is.

Sandy: Why?

Julie: Well, yesterday evening I was out walking and I used that line on a couple of people. *(Julie walks away from Sandy to show her what happened and the past takes place. Laura walks in.)*

Julie *(without feeling):* Hi, Laura. How are you?

Laura *(without feeling and looking down):* Just fine, thank you. How are you?

Julie *(without feeling):* Just fine, thank you.

(Laura walks off and Gary walks on.)

Julie: How are you?

Gary *(instantly falls on one knee and clutches Julie's hand):* Oh, my day has been horrible, unbelievable! I'm *so* glad you asked!

Julie *(startled):* Sir, I . . . .

Gary: The day started when I woke up this morning.

Julie *(trying to get away):* Sir, I really have to . . . .

Gary *(frantically):* You don't care about me!

Julie: No, uh, I mean, *yes*, I do. I was going to say that I'd really love to, *(looks around embarrassedly):* uh, hear your whole story. *(She gestures to the chairs.)* Please, have a seat. *(Both sit on the chairs.)*

Gary: Well, I woke up to this wild screaming. My talking parakeet was dying. I held it in my hand and its last gasping, shivering words were, *(talks like a parakeet):* "I'm in pain." It must have been in awful pain because I never taught it to say that. Then I went outside to bury it and I stepped on a rake. It hit me on the head, knocking me unconscious. When I woke up, a bunch of stray dogs had evidently eaten my bird and were licking me in the face. I ran in the house, looked at the clock and discovered I had been unconscious for two hours. I was late! I got dressed as fast as I could, rushed to the airport, and found that my plane had taken off without me. To make matters even worse, it crashed!

Julie: Well, you should be thankful that you weren't on it.

Gary: I was the scheduled pilot; if I had been flying it like I was supposed to, maybe it wouldn't have gone down!

Julie: Oh! *(Pause.)* Was anyone hurt?

Gary: Only one person; he broke both arms, but survived.

Julie: It could have been much worse than that!

Gary: That one person was the president of the airlines. He fired me.

Julie: Oh. I'm sorry. What did you do then?

Gary: What else could I do? I started for the terminal. But as I walked across the street, a car swerved to miss me, crashed through a guardrail and sank to the bottom of the lake.

Julie: Oh no! Did the driver survive?

Gary: Yes, but I wish he hadn't.

Julie: That's an awful thing to say! Why would you say that?

Gary: He was driving my car! *(Pulls out a handkerchief and wipes his nose and eyes.)* He had stolen my car! *(He looks away.)*

Julie: Oh! *(Walks back to Sandy.)* Do you believe this story?

Sandy: All in one day?

Julie: That's not the end of it! Listen to this. *(Walks back over to Gary.)*

Gary: So I decided to go to my parent's house for a little sympathy. I had to take the bus. *(Blows his nose.)* I took the wrong bus. I ended up on the wrong side of town and started trying to find another bus to get out of there. Then I thought I got lucky because an off-duty taxi stopped when I waved to it. But the driver got out with these big, hairy, tattooed arms and *(with emphasis)* he mugged me. He took everything I had and tore my clothes. *(Wipes his eyes, sniffles.)* He also called me names.

Julie *(looks over at Sandy):* Do you believe this?

Gary: Well, I found just enough change in the gutter to catch a bus to my parent's house.

Julie *(sighing with relief):* So you finally made it home! Did your parents make you feel better?

Gary *(crying loudly):* My parents had moved! They never even told me. I couldn't believe this was happening to me! I had to walk all the way back to my place—in the cold, with torn clothes—what else could I do? What a day. I step on a rake, the plane I'm supposed to be flying crashes, I get fired, my car is destroyed, I get mugged by a guy with big tattooed arms, I get called names and I can't find my parents. Oh boy! And when I finally made it home. . . .

Julie: Oh! I bet you were glad to get there!

Gary: The plane had crashed into *my* house! Nose-dived right into my living room. What a day! *(Blows his nose.)*

Julie *(pauses):* I'm very sorry. I've never had a perfect stranger tell me of a worse day. I mean, *(pauses, looking down)* is there anything I can do?

Gary *(stands up):* No, I'll be alright.

Julie: Really. If I can help in anyway . . . .

Gary: You don't know what a help you've been just listening and caring. I feel *(with emphasis)* much better. *(Sniffing.)* I don't usually cry in front of a stranger, *(slight pause)* especially a woman.

Julie: Well, I understand. Do you need any more help?

Gary: No, I've got to go. I've got a cockpit to move out of my living room. But thanks a lot.

Julie: Sure.

(Gary exits as Julie watches him. She then walks back over to Sandy.)

Sandy: Wow, I can't believe the day that guy had!

Julie: I know; I never had any idea. I mean, I just said the usual "How are you?" *(Pause.)* But you know what? I bet there's a lot of people that we pass every day that are really hurting and we never know. We ask, but sometimes, we don't really care.

Sandy: I guess sometimes our hearts don't match what our mouths say.

Julie *(slight pause):* Sorry I got mad at you. Everything just kind of got to me.

Sandy: Hey, I understand.

Julie: Well, I'll see you later.

Sandy *(with emphasis):* Thanks for telling me about that! Bye.

(Sandy walks to center stage as Julie leaves. Laura walks on stage and she and Sandy pass by each other. Sandy turns around to face Laura.)

Sandy *(sincerely):* How are you?

Laura *(quickly and without feeling)* Just fine, thanks.

Sandy *(takes a few steps toward Laura):* No, really. *(Laura stops and looks at Sandy, who repeats sincerely):* How are you?

Laura *(stops and smiles at Sandy):* I'm much better! Thanks for asking!

(Both smile at each other and continue on their ways.)

Curtain

Characters

Roger, a young, impetuous angel
Phil, an older and wiser angel
Jesus, portrayed by an offstage voice and a bright light

Setting: Office in Heaven.

Props

White robes for angels
Two desks
Desk lamps, in/out baskets, whatever additional office items you choose
Map of Israel
Map of Bethlehem
Clipboard
Single, bright light to indicate the presence of Jesus. Connect the light above the stage, either to the right or left of center.
Amplification for the voice of Jesus

Scene: Two angels in charge of arranging the details for Christ's first visit to earth are seated at desks.

Phil (*studies a clipboard in his hand*): Okay now, I've studied the directives from the main office. You and I need to finalize the arrangements for the Lord's first visit to earth.

Roger (*excited*): All right! Let's have a parade! I love a parade! We'll have a big float covered with giant lilies, and a cou-

70

ple of legions of the angelic orchestra marching fore and aft! Maybe Miss Israel can ride up front, waving at everyone—you know how they do!

Phil *(cutting in):* No, Roger, we'll have none of that stuff. We are to make His arrival simple; no frills.

Roger: All right, maybe cut the lilies....

Phil: Forget *all* of it! Now listen. First we have to figure out where He will arrive ....

Roger: Oh yeah! Let's have Him appear in downtown Jerusalem! Right at high noon when everyone's out in the streets. We'll arrange a huge flash of lightning, and then—

Phil: No, no! All wrong! First of all, Jerusalem is not the right city.

Roger: Not Jerusalem? But that's where all the action is! Jerusalem is the hub, it's where things are happening!

Phil: None of that matters. The town has already been prophesied. It will be Bethlehem.

Roger: Bethlehem?!

Phil: Yeah. You know, the City of David? And another thing, He won't be "appearing" in any flash of light—He's gonna be born.

Roger: Oh yeah, that's right. He's gonna be born to that peasant couple, uh... Joseph and Myrna.

Phil: That's Joseph and Mary. I wish you would go to the staff meetings once in a while, then you would know this stuff!

Roger: Oh Phil, quit harping.

Phil: I can't help it, I'm an angel.

Roger: Okay, okay. So it's gonna be Bethlehem. But Joseph and Mary live in Nazareth. How're we gonna get them to Bethlehem?

Phil: We discussed *that* at the staff meeting too! It's simple—Joseph has to go there to be taxed.

Roger: Oh, good old taxation. *(Pause.)* If only Adam and Eve hadn't eaten from that tree.... Hey! What kind of tax forms do the Romans use? The 1040?

Phil: No, the Roman form is called the 10-4.

Roger: Is it simple?

Phil: Very. The Roman soldier says, "Gimme a fourth of your income," and you say, "10-4!"

Roger: I see. Okay, so we've gotten Joseph and Mary to Bethlehem. Now let's find them a really prime place to stay. *(He gets up and unrolls a map of Bethlehem.)* Here's a great place; the Bethlehem Hilton! They've got heated Jacuzzis and twenty-four-hour room service! We can hang a big banner in the lobby welcoming the King, and have a *heavenly* choir! The parade can start there and end up down here *(he indicates on the map)* on Fig Avenue—

Phil *(impatient):* I told you, no parade! What's more, the hotels are all booked.

Roger: All booked? All booked! You mean to tell me the King of kings is going to earth and those people won't even give Him a room in a hotel? Why is Bethlehem so crowded anyway? Because of holiday shopping?

Phil *(getting angry):* No! I told you, taxation!

Roger: Well, if they can't throw Him a parade, at *least* a few of them could agree to sleep in the lobby! *(Pause.)* Boy, I wish we could have a parade—I really love a parade!

Phil: I've picked up on that. Now, since there's no room in the inn, I've arranged for Him to be born in a barn.

Roger *(stunned):* A barn? *(Then he smiles.)* Oh, a *barn!* I get it—you're joking! Boy, Phil, you really know how to keep a straight face—for a second there, I thought you were serious! A barn—ha!

Phil: I am serious. The Lord of Heaven will be born in a barn.

Roger: What?? Oh, you've really lost it this time, Phil. You've gone too far. I can maybe go along with these other details, but this—this is too much. You're gonna get laughed—or chased—right out of Heaven!

Phil: A barn fits with the directives I was given.

Roger *(sarcastically):* Oh, and I suppose the directives call for straw and goats and chickens and donkeys! Picture it, the cattle are lowing, the poor baby wakes—

Phil: "Lowing?" What's lowing? I thought cows mooed.

Roger: I don't know, I heard it in a song somewhere. But never mind that! Where's the baby gonna sleep? *(Sarcastically):* In a manger?

Phil *(checks his notes):* Yeah, that's what I have written down.

Roger *(covers his face):* Oh, angel! I can just hear all the jokes that are gonna come out of this; "How's your baby, Mary?" "Oh, he's in stable condition." Oh, you've blown it this time, for sure!

Phil: I don't think so. But, let's get on with the planning. We also have to come up with the people who will be notified of our Lord's birth, who will come to worship Him and then spread the news.

Roger *(getting back to business):* Okay, okay. Let's see. *(Goes to map.)* The Bethlehem Country Club is pretty close, and we'll definitely have to contact the Pharisees. Let's get the influential citizens out to greet him... since we can't have a parade. But Phil! I can promise you that the leading citizens of Bethlehem are not gonna want to troop out to some stable! That is *not* a good idea!

Phil: Forget the Pharisees and influential citizens. I was thinking of contacting some shepherds. *(He goes to the map.)* See? There will be a little group of them out on these hills that night—we can put on a full-light angelic display—you ought to like *that* idea!

Roger *(stunned again):* Shepherds?! You're gonna let *them* be the messengers? *(Getting very serious.)* Phil, nobody will let them in their houses, let alone listen to them! Shepherds are a strange bunch of guys! They talk, and *sing* to sheep! And do you know what else?

Phil: What, Roger?

Roger: They *smell* like sheep! *(He fans his nose.)* Yucch! Have you smelled a shepherd lately? Who's gonna believe *anything* they have to say?

Phil: Well... I also thought we could summon some Persian astrologers to come over. They've been studying Hebrew prophecy and watching the skies for a sign. We could give them one! The trip would take them some time, but we could put a star overhead to guide them, and...

Roger *(putting an arm around Phil condescendingly):* Phil, Phil, Phil.... Let me review this with you. The Son of God will take the form of a helpless baby, to be born to two obscure peasants. He'll arrive in a nowhere town because of taxation, and be born in a barn, and sleep in a manger.

Phil *(excitedly):* And He'll be wrapped in swaddling clothes!

Roger: And the only people we'll be contacting will be a bunch of stinky shepherds and some foreigners?

Phil: Right!

Roger *(sadly):* Phil, we've been friends a long time...seems like forever... but I gotta tell you, the sap is no longer flowing to your top branches.

(Jesus—the bright light—enters. The two angels bow in unison to one knee. During this scene, the actors playing Roger and Phil should be careful that they do not look at and speak to the spot of light on the floor, but to the column of light—Jesus is at least as tall as they are.)

Both: Greetings, Lord!

Jesus: Relax, fellows. How are you doing with the plans for my birth? Do you have the details worked out?

Roger: Oh, Lord! Wait'll You hear the plans Phil came up with!

Jesus: Okay. *(He waits. When Phil and Roger only look at each other in puzzlement, Jesus patiently asks,)* Have you located a good place for my birth?

(Phil starts to speak but Roger cuts him off.)

Roger: Get this! *He* wants You to be born in a stable and sleep in a manger!

Jesus *(considering this):* Hummm. How about the people you will contact?

(Again, Phil starts to speak and Roger cuts him off.)

Roger *(thumbing to Phil):* He wants to go with—can You believe this?—shepherds and Eastern astrologers!!

Phil: Well, Lord, what do You think?

Roger *(shaking his head):* I'll start cleaning out his desk right now. *(He moves toward the desk.)*

Jesus: I think your plans are great!

Roger *(stops suddenly):* What??

Jesus: Your plans are great, Phil! You followed our directives very well.

Phil: Thank You, my Lord.

Roger: Ummm... just out of curiosity, Lord... don't You think this approach will turn off the respectable people?

Jesus: No, only the proud.

Roger: But... but... You're the Son of God! Don't You deserve the best?

Jesus: Of course, that goes without saying. But if I insist on getting what I deserve, all the humans will get what they deserve. And, if I'm going to earth, it's best that I slip in without a whole lot of hoopla.

Roger *(brownnosing):* Yes, of course, Lord... *(completely puzzled):* but, *why?*

Jesus: If I come in meekness, only the wise and the humble will seek me.

Roger *(completely bewildered):* But Lord, aren't you going to lose a lot of people that way?

Jesus *(sadly):* Yes. Those who seek a savior for the wrong reasons will be lost. But, this is the only form in which I should visit earth—until the end, of course. In fact, even after I ascend from earth, I will continue to visit in the form of poor peasants, down-trodden old folks, obscure shut-ins, and others who are rejected by their fellowman. I'll visit the dirt farms of Haiti, the villages of Asia and Africa, Harlem in New York, or maybe *(fill in the name of the poor section of your town).* That way, those who minister to the least of my brothers, will be ministering to me.

Roger *(slowly, beginning to understand):* The only people who will notice You will be...

Roger and Phil: ...the humble and the wise!

Jesus *(kindly):* That's right!

Roger: I guess I understand, but Lord, you oughta know something....

Jesus: What's that?

Roger: You're never gonna get a parade this way!

(Optional)
Jesus: Someday I will, Roger. Someday....

Curtain

Joint-Heir Force

Characters

    Sgt. Caruso, stern, sincere military type. May be male or female

    Elli Burndish (or Eli, depending on gender); dingy, happy-go-lucky, uncommitted

Setting

    The office of the Joint-Heir Force (Lord's Army) recruiting station. Three chairs are all that are necessary, but you may wish to elaborate with a desk, and military recruitment (and/or travel) posters on the walls.

Props/Costumes

    Military hat for sergeant, or entire uniform
    Burndish may be dressed sloppily
    Desk, chairs, posters

Performance Tips

If Burndish and Caruso are played by actors/actresses of the opposite sex, then the line, "Maybe even a little romance," can be delivered flirtatiously.

Scene: *A recruiting station. The recruiter, Sergeant Caruso, is nodding off behind the desk when Elli Burndish walks onstage.*

Elli *(entering from either side, reviewing written directions):* Let's see . . . second door on the left, after the third hallway, up from the lavender stairwell, in the second building, three blocks over from the fifth bridge, go nine blocks and turn green. Hmmm . . . oh, this must be it—"Lord's Army Recruiting Station." *(Walks closer to center and knocks.)* Hello?! Yoo hoo! You at the desk—you gotta recruit!

Sergeant Caruso: What? Oh, oh, come in, come in. I'm Sgt. Caruso. Have a seat. *(He indicates one of the two chairs.)* Don't sit in that one: it slopes downhill and it's well-waxed. It's for traveling office-upply salesmen.

Elli *(sits down):* Hey, I didn't mean to interrupt your midafternoon siesta . . . or were you inspecting the insides of your eyelids?

Sgt. Caruso: No, no . . . just hard to stay awake sometimes . . . especially since our coffee machine is broken.

Elli: Broken? Why don't you sue the company?

Sgt. Caruso: On what grounds? *(Then together with Elli:)* Coffee grounds! *(They both chuckle.)* It's just that things have been kind of slow around here lately.

Elli: What's the problem?

Sgt. Caruso: Just don't get many recruits these days. I suppose being on the "Joint-Heir Force" doesn't have the same appeal as it used to.

Elli: "Joint-Heir Force?"

Sgt. Caruso: You know, "Joint-Heirs With Christ"—a force of individuals dedicated to doing the work of Christ—"Joint-Heir Force." Anyway, there aren't many recruits, and the ones we *do* get . . .

Elli: Well, that's what I'm here for, Sgt. Calypso.

Sgt. Caruso: That's Caruso.

Elli: Yeah, well, I'd like to volunteer for God's Army—or "Joint-Heir Force," if you prefer.

Sgt. Caruso *(getting excited):* Certainly, certainly. Uh, what's your name?

Elli: Elli Burndish.

Sgt. Caruso: Yes, Elli, we'd love to have you. I'll fill out a form right away. *(He goes to a file—real or imaginary—or pulls open a desk drawer.)*

Elli: Oh, that quick, huh? Like . . . don't I have to get a physical or anything?

Sgt. Caruso: No, once you're enlisted, we've got some definite restrictions. But as far as signing up goes, we'll take you as you come.

Elli: "Just as I am without one plea"—that sort of thing?

Sgt. Caruso: You've got it!

Elli: Boy, you guys must be desperate.

Sgt. Caruso *(indignant):* We're not desperate, Burndish. Our only requirement is the willingness to serve. If you've got that, the commander has an uncanny ability to *make* you super-effective.

Elli: I see. Well, let's get started. I'm willing *and* able. I've got some references here and a list of my credentials . . .

Sgt. Caruso: *No* previous experience is necessary. In fact, we don't care about your abilities or credentials, because doubtless they aren't good enough. The only way anyone can get into this army is by the goodness of the commander, whose policy is, "Fulfill the future and forget the past."

Elli: Well . . . e x c u s e me!

Sgt. Caruso *(filling out a form):* Okay, Elli. I need some information from you.

Elli: Shoot.

Sgt. Caruso: What got you interested in the Lord's army—a sermon?

Elli: No, that stuff turns me off. It was a poster I saw. It simply said, "J-E-S-U-S' Army Wants You!" And in the background of the poster you could see smiling faces, beautiful scenery, and exciting adventure. I said to myself, right then and there, "Burndish, this is where you belong!" Just think of all the benefits!

Sgt. Caruso *(lowers his pen and looks up):* Benefits, huh?

Elli: Sure, something to work for! The social life—maybe a little romance. *And,* I heard the commander blesses the socks off of you financially.

Sgt. Caruso: You've been watching the wrong channel, buds. So you're in it for the benefits, huh? How about the joy of serving under the commander?

Elli: Huh? Oh yeah, yeah—that too.

Sgt. Caruso: Now, there are a few things you should know, Burndish. There's a rigorous training program you'll need to go through to be a good soldier.

Elli: Rigorous training? For how long?

Sgt. Caruso: You never stop training. You must devote time for speaking with the Commander, studying His strategy manual, and time to gather with other troops to pledge your allegiance to Him.

Elli: Sounds pretty radical to me.

Sgt. Caruso: It is.

Elli: Well, listen, I'll try to fit these things into my schedule, if I can.

Sgt. Caruso: They're not optional. When you join with Him, His schedule becomes *your* schedule.

Elli: Hey, listen, Sergeant, this harsh approach isn't gonna appeal to very many . . .

Sgt. Caruso: If you want to "win friends and influence people," go to a Dale Carnegie Course.

Elli: Well, when do these troop gatherings take place? They don't sound so bad.

Sgt. Caruso: That depends on your local platoon. But, most of them meet on Sunday mornings, around 9:30.

Elli: Sunday mornings?!

Sgt. Caruso: Yup.

Elli: You mean, like the Sunday morning after Saturday night?

Sgt. Caruso: That's the one.

Elli: Saturday nights with late parties?

Sgt. Caruso: Hold it just one minute! I don't know what parties you're talking about, but most I know of are not consistent with the Commander's image.

Elli: What? You mean I gotta do everything like Him?

Sgt. Caruso: If you wanna be a soldier in His army, you do.

Elli: I'll be like a little clone of Him running around?

Sgt. Caruso: That's not a bad way of putting it.

Elli: Well, tell me about the retirement plan. I heard it's really great!

Sgt. Caruso: It's out of this world! *(Elli starts to dream.)* But only to those who fight to the death.

Elli *(sits up in surprise):* What?! What fighting?!

Sgt. Caruso: What fighting? Fighting to win the hearts of people over to the Commander's control. What did you think soldiers did—plant tulips?

Elli: Well, I knew some people fought, but golly! What does this fighting involve?

Sgt. Caruso: Confront the people around you with their need to submit to the Commander's control!

Elli: Confront people?! I don't want to cramp anyone's style, including my own! Now what do you say we strike a deal?

Sgt. Caruso: Like what?

Elli: Like . . . put me down for partial commitment . . . .

Sgt. Caruso: No such thing.

Elli: *Sometimes* talk to the Commander, *sometimes* read the strategy manual and *sometimes* go to troop gatherings. *If* I can make it, and *if* they don't get fanatical when they pledge their allegiance to Him.

Sgt. Caruso: They do.

Elli: And I'll live like the Commander would, except when it's inconvenient or embarrassing, and *no* fighting!

Sgt. Caruso: *A soldier who doesn't fight?*

Elli: Well, I don't want to impose *His* values on anyone or condemn anyone's lifestyle. But I like those benefits . . .

Sgt. Caruso: That's too bad. Listen, Burndish, I think I know where you belong. *(He goes to file or opens drawer and pulls out another form.)*

Elli: Where?

Sgt. Caruso: In another army entirely—The Lukewarm Corps.

Elli: Lukewarm? Hmmm . . . well, I wouldn't quite put it that way, but okay—The Lukewarm Corps.

Sgt. Caruso *(hands Elli a form):* Here. You'll be fighting under a different commander.

Elli: *(reading form):* Hmmmm . . . General Beelzebub . . . that's a weird name. *(She gets up to leave.)*

Sgt. Caruso: He's a weird guy. But his soldiers like him 'cause he lets them do as they please . . . at first . . .

Elli: Sounds great! Wow! I've only been signed up for five minutes and I'm already being transferred!

Sgt. Caruso: That's one way of putting it.

Elli: What's another way?

Sgt. Caruso: The Commander calls it spewing you out of His mouth. *(They freeze.)*

Curtain

Just Like Peter

Characters
Jill, intelligent young Christian
Joe, energetic, nice young Christian
Judy, not too smart, but friendly, also a Christian
Millie, Chemistry wiz, very brainy, likes Joe
Bart, dream-guy type, Jill's boyfriend, a little conceited

Setting
A high-school hallway.

Props/Costumes
A dollar bill
Two wallet-sized pictures
School books and notebooks
Prerecorded sound of a rooster crowing
Prerecorded reading of Jesus' warning to Peter, or have some-
one in the background ready with a mike

Performance Tips
Bart's dropping of the dollar bill should seem accidental. This
can be done by having the dollar between two books, which he
shuffles as he walks past Joe.

It's important to obtain the sound of a real rooster crowing.
This keeps the final scene dramatic and not comical.

Scene: *Judy and Jill are center stage talking quietly. Joe comes
up behind them to join them. All three are carrying books.*

Joe *(energetic, good-natured):* Good morning, Christian babes!

Jill *(friendly):* Hi, Joe.

Judy *(nice):* Morning.

Joe: Is everyone ready for another week of high-school fun?

Jill *(faking boredom):* Next question please.

Judy *(trying to change the subject):* Good Bible study last night,
wasn't it?

Jill: Yeah, I just wish the others would be more quiet.

Joe: I heard that! I'm really starting to get into it, but sometimes I can hardly hear with all the talking.

Jill: Maybe we could confer with the teacher or something.

Judy: *Or,* maybe we could tell the teacher.

(Jill and Joe exchange a look—with half smiles.)

Joe: Did you read the verses for next week's lesson on Peter?

Jill: You bet.

Judy: I did!

Joe: It's hard to believe that Peter could have blown it like he did; he denied Jesus!

Judy: I know. How could he have done that?

Joe: He'd seen Jesus do all those miracles and heard all that He had said—and even talked directly to Him!

Jill: And Jesus was being beaten by the soldiers while Peter was denying that he knew Him! *(Indignant):* Peter was a disciple! He was actually in the vicinity of Jesus for years!

Judy: And he was with Jesus, too.

Joe *(winces):* Right. *(Turns back to Jill):* I could never say "I don't know Jesus." I mean, to just out and out deny Him—

Judy: I know. Jesus even told Peter that he would deny Him.

Joe: But he did it anyway, and then the rooster crowed, and Peter realized what he had done.

Judy: The sound of that rooster crowing must have been sad for Peter to hear, huh?

Jill: Yeah. *(Short pause, thinking.)* I think it's easier today, for us to remain loyal to Jesus. We probably wouldn't get stabbed with a sword in school if we talked about Him.

Joe: But we're not allowed to pray! Not publicly, anyway.

Jill: But we wouldn't be incarcerated if we did.

Judy: We wouldn't get put in prison either.

Joe & Jill *(look at Judy, then at each other in amazement):* Yeah, right.

Joe: I guess you're right, it is easier for us today. But still, Peter *was* a disciple, and he blew it.

Jill: I feel like I've come to the place as a Christian where I could never deny Jesus. Not anymore.

Joe: Me too.

Judy: I know what you mean, I feel that way too. I just wish the rest of the youth group felt that way.

Joe: Yeah, that would be great. *(Pause)* So, Judy, are you ready for your chemistry test?

Judy: Oh no! Rocks for brains! I forgot! What am I gonna do? I really need a good grade on this one! *(Looks away, distressed.)*

(Millie walks up to the group.)

Joe: Hi, Millie.

Millie *(ignores the girls, flirts with Joe):* Hi, Joe.

Judy *(hasn't seen Millie, is talking about herself):* What a jerk!

Millie *(thinks Judy's comment was meant for her):* Thanks a lot! *(Walks angrily away stage left and stops with arms folded around her books, looking away from the group.)*

Judy *(turns toward Millie):* No, not you! *(Looks back at Joe and Jill)* Ohhhhhh! I've got an idea! *(Points to Millie):* The chemistry wiz!

(Judy rushes over to Millie, Joe and Jill talk silently.)

Judy: Millie wait!

Millie *(looking over her shoulder, hurt)*: Thanks a lot! Jerk, huh?

Judy: No, *I'm* the jerk; I forgot about the chemistry test today. Are you ready?

Millie *(turning around)*: Of course. *(Proudly)*: I've memorized the entire periodic table.

Judy: The what?

Millie: The list of all the chemical elements.

Judy: Huh?

Millie *(slowly and patiently)*: Judy, I've memorized and am able to write down everything I need to know for the test.

Judy: Oh! *(Short pause.)* Millie, I need help. Do you have the list with you?

Millie: Yes, but this is not an open-book quiz; we're not allowed to use our notes.

Judy: Oh yeah... right.

Millie: I suppose you could cheat.

Judy: Oh, I don't know. I. . . .

Millie: Well, it's no big deal to just sneak a look at someone else's notes!

Judy: Well—uh, oh. . . no, I guess not. Especially when my whole grade depends on this test!

Millie: Okay, start cramming. *(Pulls out notes, hands them to Judy, and says proudly)*: Of course, it all comes easy to me.

(They walk on silently, looking at the notes. Bart enters from stage right.)

Jill *(excitedly)*: Oh, there's Bart. I'll see you later, Joe. *(Walks over to Bart, Joe looks at his notes.)*

Bart: Hi, Jill! You look nice today.

Jill: Thanks. *(Takes Bart's hand.)* You look pretty good yourself.

Bart: Thanks, I know I do. So, do you want a copy of my class photo?

Jill: Yes! Do you have one for me?

Bart: Sure. *(Pulls photo out of his pocket.)* Here it is, and let me tell you, I look good!

Jill: And you saved this just for me?

Bart: Well, I sold all of the ones from the school, but I had reprints made so there would be enough for everyone.

Jill: Will you sign it for me, please?

Bart: Come on, you know I hate that! *(Pause.)* Did you get your pictures?

Jill: Yes, but they're horrible!

Bart: Let me see.

Jill *(takes picture out of her purse)*: Here, don't laugh.

Bart: Hey, "you look maaarveeelous."

Jill: Thanks.

Bart *(tucks photo into his shirt pocket)*: How about skipping English to spend some time with me?

Jill: How?

Bart: Tell Mr. (   ) that you've got to go to the bathroom, but instead, come out here and see me.

Jill: I don't know. . . *(questioning)*: I'd have to lie.

Bart: Oh, come on! *(Pours on the charm):* I really want to see you. I *need* to see you. Come on, whaddya say? Listen, if you come to see me, I'll write something on the back of that picture that you'll never forget! *(Gives her a seductive look.)*

Jill: Well. . . okay.

Bart: Good! Now remember, use the bathroom excuse; it works every time! See ya later!

Jill: Bye, Bart. *(Looks down at picture, smiling.)*

(As Bart exits, stage left, he crosses in front of Joe and accidently drops a dollar bill. Joe sees it, picks it up and starts to call after Bart. Instead, he looks at the bill and stuffs it in his pocket. Jill's eyes have been on Bart's picture, and she sees none of this. Jill walks over to Joe, center stage, still clutching Bart's picture.)

Joe: I feel sorry for Judy—forgetting to study for the test.

Jill: Yeah, well, I don't know that studying would help her much!

Joe *(laughs):* Yeah, I know what you mean! *(Jill laughs too.)*

(Judy, with sheet in hand, leaves Millie [who exits stage left] and walks over to join Joe and Jill.)

Judy: What are you two laughing about?

(Just then, they all hear the sound of a rooster crowing, and they all react in shock.)

Joe *(unbelieving):* Did—did you guys hear that? It—

Voice *(over the PA system):* Before the rooster crows, you will deny me three times.

(Judy looks at the study sheet, Jill looks at Bart's picture, Joe pulls the dollar out of his pocket and looks at it. Then they all look sadly at each other and hang their heads.)

Curtain

Let's Fake a Deal

Characters
Angel #1, a little depressed
Angel #2, the same
Matt Terial, game show host, fast talking and confident
Flip Hummel, nervous but intelligent, excitable
Johnny, crowd man and game-show voice, fast talking and direct

Setting
Heaven, and a game show set on earth. Since we can't begin to portray Heaven, the setting comes from the dialogue and the audience's imagination.

Props/Costumes
Two chairs
Two angel costumes; white sheets and halos
Turnip costume, a loosely-hung sheet and green headdress
Cue cards, "Cheer," "Laugh," "Wow," "Ooooh!," "Hummm," "The Cross," "The Prizes," "Cheer if you're a Christian."
Upbeat theme music for game show, relaxed prize background music

Performance Tips
The cue cards involve the audience. You can present the skit without them, but they add to the game-show atmosphere. Flash each card long enough to get a response, but don't drag it out. Characters should wait until audience can hear before delivering the next line.

Costumes can be elaborate to add to the visual effect, or really bad for extra comedy. Theme music helps to create excitement.

All earth action should be center and stage left, while Heaven is stage right. Keep the actions separated so the audience won't be confused.

Scene: *Two chairs are on the right, angled slightly toward center stage. The two angels walk in and sit down. They are a little depressed.*

Angel 1: Boy, I sure could go for a little rejoicing here in Heaven.

Angel 2: Yeah, me too. *(With a little more excitement):* I brought the party favors—the hats and uh, the noisemakers—just in case somebody comes to the Lord.

Angel 1: I hope we get to use them.

Angel 2 *(less depressed):* Last time we had a good bash was when *(name of local minister)* finally got some of that sin out of his life.

Angel 1: That sure was a long time in coming, huh? Say, how long ago was that—in earth time?

Angel 2: A couple of days ago.

Angel 1: Oh, yeah.

Angel 2 *(pauses, thinking):* Hey, *(more excited)* I've got an idea; let's look down on that game show!

Angel 1 *(more excited):* Do you mean, "Let's Fake a Deal?"

Angel 2: Yeah! Flip Hummel is gonna be on. He's been seriously considering following Jesus for two weeks—earth time of course.

Angel 1 *(happy and excited):* There could be some rejoicing!

Angel 2: I hope so, for Heaven's sake!

Angel 1: For his sake, too!

Angel 2: Of course! *(Both angels look stage left.)*

Johnny *(enters from the left, stands center stage):* Good evening ladies and gentlemen. Before the actual show begins, I'd like to welcome you. I'm Johnny, the crowd-cue guy and I need your help. In order for any show to be as great as our show is, it needs an enthusiastic and loud audience; you are the ones who really make the show. So, when I hold up a cue card, you need to give me all you've got. *(Goes through cue cards with audience, encouraging them to do well. The angels participate too.)* All right, the show is about to start. *(Holds up "cheer" card.)* Five seconds to air time, ... four... three... two... one! *(Music starts.)* It's time for America's number one game show—"Let's Fake A Deal!" And here's your ramblin' gamblin' host, Matt Terial. *(More "cheer" card.)*

(Angels signify to each other that they don't think Matt is so great. Johnny moves to far stage left.)

Matt *(takes center stage position, is very energetic):* Welcome, welcome to "Let's Fake a Deal"—the show where everyone wins—depending on your definition of the word "win." Ha! Ha! Ha! *(Johnny holds up "laugh" card.)* Let's bring out our first contestant now. *(Flip enters.)* What's your name?

Flip *(nervously):* Flip Hummel.

Matt: Nice costume!

Flip: I'm a turnip!

Matt: Flip, what do you do for a living?

Flip: Currently, I'm in sales; I sell vegetables.

Matt: That must be why you're dressed as a turnip.

Flip *(starting to gain composure):* Exactly.

Matt: Well Flip, we're glad you could—"turn-up" on our program today. Ha! Ha! Ha!

(Johnny holds up the "laugh" cue card.)

Flip: Glad to be here.

Matt *(sarcastically):* You bet. Well—*(nicer)* you, Flip, get to choose between whatever is behind curtain #1 or curtain #2, or you could sign this ticket stub *(takes ticket out of his pocket)* and be eligible to win a lifetime supply of nose-hair removers. As soon as one wears out, we'll replace it at no charge. Do you understand the choices Flip?

Flip: Yes, but why . . . .

Matt *(cutting Flip off):* What'll it be?

(Johnny holds up "Cheer" cue card.)

Flip: I'll go for the curtains!

(Cue card, "Cheer.")

Matt: He's gonna go for the curtains! He's gonna "flip" for curtain number one! Ha! Ha! Ha! Here's Johnny to tell you about it. *(Prize background music starts)*

Johnny *(holds up "wow" card):* That's right, the package behind curtain number one starts off with a new boat! No more landlubbing when you have this twenty-foot cruiser from Bob & Float! And that's not all, there's much, much, more! *(Speaks faster):* It's a new car! *(Holds up "ooooh" card.)* An '87 corvette fresh off the line, also, a condominium on the French Riviera, two plane tickets for anywhere in this great world, $100,000 in cash, a $10,000 diamond pendant, a mink coat, a $4,000 shopping spree at the store of your choice, an Italian racing bike, dinner with the President, and an all-expense-paid trip to see Rock City! What a great prize package! *(Out of breath, holds up "Cheer" card.)*

Matt: How about curtain number two? *(Music starts.)*

Johnny: *(less excited):* That's right, behind curtain number two is a cross. *(holds up "hummm" card, Angels grin at each other and give the thumbs up signal, nod their approval to Flip.)* You can carry it everywhere—it comes equipped with it's own shoulder strap. But that's not all—it has a promise from Jesus Christ to help you carry it. And—you will have abundant life here and now as well as eternal life in Heaven, where you'll walk streets of gold, never cry or experience pain, and be personally loved by God forever. It's a cross to carry, and a promise of eternal happiness! *(Holds up "Hummm" card.)*

Matt: Well, what'll it be? Curtain number one with all those fabulous prizes—just think about laying your hands on them—*(sarcastically):* or curtain number two with the cross and the I.O.U. from God? You've got twenty seconds to make your choice.

Angel 1 *(cheering):* Come on Flip! Eternity is at stake!

Angel 2: The cross, the cross!

Flip: All those prizes. . . look pretty good. . . .

(Johnny holds up "cheer" card.)

Flip: A cross. . . a promise from God . . . .

(Angels hold up their own card saying "Cheer if you're a Christian.")

Flip: I just can't decide. A boat, a car, a condominium. . . loved by God forever. . . .

Matt: Come on Flip, ten seconds now. A cross and an I.O.U.? *(Angels flash "the cross" card, Johnny flashes "prizes" card.)* Come on, think about laying your hands on those prizes. They may not last, but they're fun while you have them.

Flip: Don't last? Loved by God forever? I'll take the cross!

Matt *(disappointed):* Oh, I can't believe it! *(Angels jump up and down with the "cheer" card and rejoice. Theme music comes on. Angels go down and meet Flip and take him toward the cross. All are excited.)*

Matt: Well, sorry folks, that's our show for today. This is Matt Terial for "Let's Fake a Deal." See you next week! *(As he's walking off, he questions Johnny):* Why would he choose the cross? Talk about throwing away your future! *(They walk off, depressed.)*

Curtain

On the Other Side of the Glass

Characters: Three Goldfish
   Hook, very satisfied, intelligent
   Line, also content, but not too bright
   Sinker, nervous, impatient, searching

Setting
   The inside of a fish tank. Except for references to the environment in the script and possible fishy costumes, the set is left to the imagination of the audience. Having unquestionable boundries to the tank will help the audience visualize a tank. Place tape marks on the floor that the audience will not see. The fish will circle the circumfrence of this space and butt against the side, but *never* cross the lines.

Costumes
   Bright, goldfish-colored sweat suits
   Fins for arms, backs, and heads (optional)

Performance Tips
   Characters don't have to be in costumes, but costumes will help the effect. If the actors wish, they can make the occasional "fish mouth" movement (suck in cheeks, open and close pursed lips). If fins are not used, actors should either keep their hands in their pockets, or curl arms up to resemble fins.
   The scenes where Hook and Line are watching Sinker should be well-rehearsed so that their heads and eyes move in unison. (You might also consider having someone hidden from the audience's view gesturing to indicate Sinker's movements so that Hook and Line may follow the movement with their eyes.)

Scene: *Hook and Line are drifting lazily around, looking out of the tank toward the audience.*

Hook *(takes a deep, contented breath):*   Sure is nice here! It's great to be a fish!

Line *(also content):*   Yeah! Our life is neat!

Hook: We've got a nice big tank with plenty of clean water. *(Line smiles dreamily and nods his agreement.)* We've got big bubbles for air. *(Line looks up and around to see bubbles, smiles and nods.)* We've got clean glass to look through. *(Line* *stretches out a fin to touch glass, smiles and nods.)* And every day we get yummy, flaky, smelly food without doing any hunting or foraging!

Line *(rubs his/her stomach, smiles bigger, and nods some more.)* Well, *almost* every day!

Hook: Yeah, right. And to top it all off, we've got great fake plastic plants to swim around!

Line: *(nodding his/her head in agreement):* We've even got an ever-changing view of the kid's room! *(Points outside the tank):* Sometimes it's clean, most times, it's not, but it's always interesting! Life couldn't be much better, could it?

Hook: I can't see how.

Line: Do you remember how we felt the day we came here?

Hook: Fish, I'll never forget! That was the worst day of my life!

Line: Yeah. Those giant people grabbed us out of the mother tank with a net and tossed us into little plastic bag! That's where you and I met!

Hook: That's right. And remember? That bag had a leak!

Line: Yeah! You had to grab me by the gills to save me from draining right through that hole! That was scary!

Hook: Troubled times indeed. *(Takes a deep breath):* But *this* is the life! The *good* life!

(Sinker enters, frowning.)

Line *(looking toward Sinker and pointing):* Here swims Sinker.

Sinker *(gruffly acknowledges the other two):* Hook. *(Hook waves a fin.)* Line.

Hook and Line: Sinker.

Sinker: Let me guess. You two are floating around bubbling about how great life is in this tank!

Hook: Hey! How'd you guess?

Sinker: Ha! That's what you're *always* doing! Frankly *(glaring)* I'm getting a little tired of your attitude, tired of you two, and tired of this glass cage!

Hook: Cage?! What do you mean?

Sinker: I mean, I want to jump out of here!

Hook and Line *(horrified):* What?!

Hook: Why— why— why— you *must* be joking!

Line: Sure he's joking! *(Laughs, but suddenly stops.)* You are, aren't you?

Sinker: No, I'm dead serious. *(Scowls at them.)*

Line *(to Hook):* He's not joking?

Hook: He's as serious as a fish fry.

Sinker: You bet I am. *(Puffs out his chest):* I'm goin' out there! *(Points outside the tank while Hook and Line look at each other in horror.)* Yeah, I'm going out into the kid's bedroom!

Hook *(excited):* You can't do that! Didn't your parents tell you that you'd die out there?

Line: My dad told me that the breathing of air means death!

Hook: That's right. Our elders have always taught us that "The tank is small but leads to life."

Line: Besides, the law says we can't jump out—it's a sin!

Sinker *(laughs):* Ahhh! Are you fish brains gonna swallow that line? Our parents just feed us that to keep us from having any fun! I'll bet life is a blast on the other side of the glass!

Hook: I don't know . . . .

Sinker: Come on, look at all they've got out there. They can *do* anything they want, and *go* anywhere they want. We're confined to this itty-bitty space inside this tank.

Line: We do have nice bubbles. And we get tasty, flaky food dropped in the water every day.

Hook: *(nudges Line):* Almost every day!

Sinker: But out there, we could raid the 'frige anytime we wanted!

Hook: I've heard that some of our fish brothers are inside that 'frige; frozen, with no heads!

Line *(shudders):* Ooooooh!

Sinker: I don't believe it for a minute! That's just a story parents tell to scare us!

Hook: I don't know. . . one time I saw the kid out there eating what he called fish sticks—

Line: Sick!

Hook: —and one of those sticks smelled just like my long-lost friend Berney. He always had such a distinctive smell . . . .

Sinker: I wouldn't believe anything that kid out there says or does. He is strange! He tried to stuff his mouth with Jello the other day, and almost choked to death.

Line: I saw that—it was pretty funny.

Hook: Well, once you get out there, how are you gonna get around? Perhaps you haven't noticed lately, but you don't have any legs.

Sinker: Hey! Those are minor details! All I know is, I'll be out there having a blast while you guys float around in here feeling content. *I* am gonna have a floppin' good time!

Line: It does sound like fun . . .

Hook *(quickly stops Line):* Are you crazy? It's against the law and it *can't* be done!

Sinker: Who says? Has anybody ever tried it before?

Hook: Yeah! A couple of fish tried leaving the tank once before, but we never saw or heard from them again. There was a rumor going around that they had joined some group called, "Mrs. Paul's."

Sinker: See? That's probably the name of some swingin' group where they really know how to have fun.

Hook *(pleading):* *Please* don't go, Sinker! You're gonna die, I just *know* you are! Sometimes life looks like it is more fun on the other side of the glass, but here we're at peace, we're taken care of. And after all, we don't have any way of knowing what life is *really* like out there. I think you should listen to the teaching of our elders.

Sinker: Hordes of fishermen couldn't keep me from jumping out! My mind is made up. So long, you party poopers—I'm outta here! *(He backs up and then makes a mad dash offstage.)*

(Hook and Line follow Sinker's progress with their eyes, turning toward the front of the stage as they speak the following lines.)

Hook: He's swimming fast!

Line: He's building up speed! *(Hook and Line's eyes follow Sinker as if he goes up and over the glass.)*

In unison: There he goes!

(Both move to center front and look down as if looking on the floor outside the tank.)

Hook: Look at him move!

Line: What's he doing?

Hook: I can't tell, *(gets serious):* but it looks like . . . .

Line: *(excited):* It looks like he's having the time of his life!

(Hook and Line's eyes follow Sinker in unison as he flops around.)

Line: He's jumpin' all over the place! Sinker *is* having a floppin' good time! I think I'll go out there too! *(Crouches down to jump.)*

Hook: Wait! *(Grabs Line.)* Wait—look!

Line *(puzzled):* What's he doing now? Looks like he's doing summersaults—look! He's getting the whole room wet! Whoa! *(Hook shakes his head sadly.)* Hey Hook! *(Suddenly concerned):* How come his eyes are bulging out like that? *(Looks closer, with more concern):* Hey, he doesn't look so good.

Hook: Look! Here comes the kid. Wow! He slipped on the water! Ouch!

Line: He sees Sinker! He's picking him up by the tail! *(Hook and Line look up as if out of the tank.)* Look at how Sinker's eyes are bulging out now!

Hook: The kid is throwing him back in the tank! *(Their eyes follow the imaginary Sinker around to the side of the stage.)* Here he comes! *(Both drop the heads down to stage level again, as Sinker comes flopping and bounding onstage.)*

Line: Look how hard he is breathing!

Sinker: *(gasping and choking):* Oh, fish!

Line: What happened? You looked like you were having a lot of fun out there!

Sinker: *(still catching his breath):* You bird brain! I was *dying* out there!

Line: *(in awe):* Wow! You're lucky the kid threw you back in!

Hook: I'll say! i guess what our parents told us *is* true; the wages of sin *are* death!

Curtain

The Orphanage

Characters

Narrator, anyone with a strong, clear voice
Egbert, honest, sincere child, very sure of his beliefs
Dad, kind and caring; a God-figure
Mr. Frizz, nice old man, slightly doddering
Kid #1, brat
Kid #2, brat
Kid #3, brat

Setting

The playground in front of an orphanage (backdrop with orphanage name over the door, or a sign that identifies the building).

Props

An identification sign for the orphanage
Chair, maybe a desk as well, for Mr. Frizz
A few toys
Hats or bows to indicate the age of the kids
For comic effect, a rumpled white wig for Mr. Frizz

Performance Tips

The narrator essentially tells this story, so it is important that the dramatic action taking place in the background does not steal all the attention away from him or her, unless it is the character's turn to speak. The ever-present children at play should remain low-key so as not to distract from the narration.

A nice comic touch, if possible, is to have Egbert leap into his father's arms when he returns.

If you use more than three other children, feel free to redistribute the six lines among them.

Scene: *Semi-ragged-looking children are playing with meager toys scattered about. Mr. Frizz, the director, is observing the children.*

Narrator: Once upon a time there was an orphanage. In it, children played and frolicked and scampered under the kind direction of Mr. Frizz. But, even though their caretaker loved them, the children were sad because they had no parents. One day, a big, shiny car pulled up to the orphanage. A man got out with his little son and approached Mr. Frizz.

Dad *(entering from left):* I'd like to leave my son, Egbert, here, please . . .

Narrator: . . . he explained.

Dad: I'm going away to build a house for us. But I will return.

Mr. Frizz: When will that be?

Dad: I'm not going to say, but I *will* return.

Narrator: With that, he gave his son, Egbert, a parting embrace and left. *(Dad exits left.)* The weeks passed and Egbert continually asserted . . .

Egbert: My father is coming to get me.

Narrator: The other children invited him to play their games, but Egbert refused, saying . . .

Egbert: No, thank you. See, my father's coming to get me.

Narrator: As the weeks turned into months, Mr. Frizz began to worry about Egbert. He feared that Egbert's father was *not* coming back and that Egbert was becoming obsessed with false hopes. One day, Mr. Frizz called Egbert in.

Mr. Frizz: Son, I'm worried about you,

Narrator: Mr. Frizz exclaimed.

Mr. Frizz: You never want to play any of the games that the other children play. Why is that?

Egbert *(innocently):* My father's coming to get me.

Mr. Frizz: Do you ever think that maybe, just maybe, your father might not come to get you?

Egbert *(conclusively):* My father *is* coming to get me!

Narrator: The months became years, and although Egbert was always friendly, he never wanted to get involved in the other children's games. He always insisted . . .

Egbert: My father *is* coming to get me.

Narrator: Often, Egbert would try to interest the other children in leaving with him when his father returned.

Egbert approaches the playing kids.

Egbert *(to kid #1):* You can come with me to my father's house!

Kid #1 *(considering the invitation):* Hummmmmm. Naw, I guess not. I'm having too much fun playing here.

Egbert sighs and walks over to kid #2.

Egbert *(to kid #2):* You can come with me to my father's house!

Kid #2: Naw, he'd probably make me follow a bunch of rules.

Egbert sadly approaches kid #3.

Egbert: *You* can come with me to my father's house, honest!

Kid #3 *(without looking up):* Buzz off!

Narrator: The other children began to jeer at Egbert, making fun of his loyalty to his father's promise. They mocked him, saying,

Kid #1: Your father's never coming back!

Kid #2: He doesn't really love you!

Kid #3: He's probably not even alive anymore!

Narrator: But Egbert didn't let them affect him. Instead, he continued to say . . .

Egbert: My father is coming to get me!

Narrator: By this time, nobody except Egbert really expected that to happen. One clear morning of a normal, routine day, Egbert's father pulled up in his shiny car.

Dad *(enters from left):* I'm here to get my son . . .

Narrator: . . .he said.

Egbert: Daddy! Daddy!

Narrator: Egbert shouted joyfully as he ran to hug his Daddy.

Egbert *(hugging his daddy tightly):* You've come to get me!

Dad: Of course I have, son. I told you I would.

Egbert and his dad start to exit, left.

Narrator: Everyone was amazed. Finally, Mr. Frizz spoke.

Mr. Frizz: Egbert, I must say, I never in a million years thought your father would come!

Narrator: Egbert happily explained . . .

Egbert *(happily and sincerely):* That's because you never knew my father!

Curtain

The Stars of Heaven

Characters

Ernest Angel, good and sincere, but with a glitzy, game show host voice

St. Johnny, offstage voice also with glitzy salesman manner

Testimonial Titan, rather hardened and street smart

Tanya the Temptation Resister, strong-willed, but proud and aloof

Selena Super-Humble, nauseatingly proud of her humility, needs to be able to sing a solo

Percy Powerhouse, exaggerated televangelist type

Handley Always, slick magician

Dr. Cyrus Rote, nerdy, nasal, monotone professor

Assistant, one who brings Tanya the nails and hammer

Tempters, waiter with a tray of cocktails, guy with a joint

Mob, at least two extra people—assistant, sickies, and tempters can all double as mob members

Sickies, three people to be "healed" by H. Always

Setting

The stage and dressing room of a game show taking place in Heaven. Divide your stage into two areas, and indicate the game show stage with a sign or banner reading, "The Stars of Heaven." Equip the dressing room with a dresser and coat rack, couch, whatever you like, but let the audience's imagination design the game show setting. (You probably can't simulate Heaven!)

Props/Costumes

Ernest, flashy suit or white suit
Tanya, high-collar, button-up puritanical dress
    cigarettes
    cans of beer
    marijuana joint
    tray of cocktails
    board with nail and hammer
Percy, huge Bible, bouffant hairdo
Handley, magician's costume
    dark sunglasses
    crutches
    cane

Performance Tips

This skit dramatizes the contrast found in 1 Corinthians 13:1-3. Make sure the performers come off as smooth artists onstage, but hideous offstage. All of the performers (onstage and off) should respond with applause at the appropriate places. Your audience may or may not join in. Because this skit is lengthy and utilizes many people, it works well as an entire evening program.

Scene 1: *Big band music is playing before and as Ernest comes running out enthusiastically to the applause of the audience.*

Ernest: Hey, hey hey! Welcome, everyone, to "The Stars of Heaven," that *celestial* talent show in which one of our contestants is going to win a *high place* of honor in Heaven! I'm your master of ceremonies, Ernest Angel. We're gathered here at Pearly Gates Auditorium to witness this event, and we have some *very* special guests in our audience tonight. Up in the balcony, supplying us with harp music, is a musical group representing the Angels of Heaven. In the mezzanine section, a little lower than the angels, are some cherubim and seraphim.

Our panel of judges this evening consists of one: the King of kings and Lord of lords, Jesus Christ. And our host for "The Stars of Heaven" tonight is none other than Jehovah, the Lord of Hosts. And now . . . let's bring on the contestants!

(The contestants all file on, grinning superficially.)

Ernest: Hello there! These people, just as they are, come from all over the earth to try to be Stars of Heaven. They're going to demonstrate their talent and try to win one of the big prizes waiting for them. But before we begin the competition, let's meet our contestants. *(Goes over to first contestant.)* Tell us your name and where you are from, please.

(Each one states his/her name and some imaginary place.)

Thank you, contestants. We remind you once again of the rules. Each one of you will put on a performance, demonstrating that you are indeed worthy of the Heavenly Grand Reward. Tell us about that reward, St. Johnny.

St. Johnny *(offstage voice):* Okay, Ernest. The Grand Reward is this beautiful mansion on the East Side of Heaven. Located on 24-Carat Avenue and overlooking the River of Life, this spacious dream house will provide an eternity of glory and praise for its maker. Designed and constructed by the Lamb Himself, this 835-room mansion contains several eternal-living rooms, large dining halls for feasting on the Bread of Life, and a kitchen-pantry complex capable of feeding 5,000.

And of course, there are no utility bills; it is lighted and heated by the glory of God. And all of it goes to the blessed winner of our "Stars of Heaven" talent pageant! Back to you, Ernest.

Ernest: Thank you, St. Johnny. Well, contestants, you've heard all about that grand reward, and I'm sure you're excited about getting started. *(To audience):* Right now, we're going to give our contestants some time in the dressing room to get ready for their big moment. But we'll be right back, so, don't go away!

107

Scene 2: *Dressing Room. All contestants file in without regard for each other's feelings or needs. As they talk, they are primping and getting ready to go back onstage.*

Testimonial Titan: I can see myself now in that great mansion, sittin' on a velvet recliner on an outdoor balcony . . . angels fannin' me with their wings . . . .

Tanya: Ha! You gotta be kidding, twit! The only way you'll ever *see* that mansion is if I invite you over—and the day I invite you over, they'll be making popsicles down there *(points to floor)* in H-E-double hockey sticks! HA! HA!

Selena: Ah, why don't you shut up! What makes you think *you're* so spiritual anyway? If you are as talented as you are good-looking, you might as well not bother going out there! I mean, is that your face, or a science project gone wrong?

Cyrus: Go ahead! You people sit back here and bicker and fight, but when that curtain comes down God'll know who the best performer was—me! Of course, it's obvious He likes *me* the best anyway. Did you see the way He smiled at me?

Handley: Smiled at you?? HA! He just couldn't keep from laughing! He probably thought you were a trained gorilla that happened to wander in!

Cyrus: Hey, jerk lips, why don't you do everyone a favor and explode? I guess you'll go out on stage and do a magic act, that is—open your mouth and make your face disappear! HA!

Percy: Hey, c'mon! I'm trying to concentrate on my performance! It's a zoo back here! You're *supposed* to be getting ready for your acts, not shooting off your traps! If brains were gasoline, you derelicts wouldn't have enough combined to transport a fruit fly's minibike around the edge of a dime!

T. Titan: What's eating you, beagle breath? Is your flea collar on too tight?

Handley: May I propose a toast? May all of you look as idiotic onstage as you do back here . . . that way I'll win the mansion without a moment's delay!

Tanya: You know something? You're not completely worthless. They could always cut off your arms and legs and use you for a paperweight!

Selena: It's a good thing I'm a God-fearing saint, or I think I'd smash a couple of your faces. Only problem is . . . I think that would improve your looks!

(General pandemonium breaks loose. Conversation explodes into hollering and screaming insults, punctuated by shoves and punches.)

All: Get out of my way! I've had about enough of you! Don't climb my frame, chump! Get lost! You make me sick! (etc.)

(Ernest appears and all suddenly freeze, then smile attentively.)

Ernest: Hey, contestants, the big moment is here! Look alive now. When it comes your turn, I'll call your name and then you come on out and do your best. May the name of the Lord be praised!

All *(in pious-sounding voices):* Amen! Hallelujah! That's right, brother! My thoughts exactly! (etc.)

(They all move offstage and Ernest returns to the center of the game show stage.)

Ernest: Well, folks, the moment of truth has arrived! Which contestant will win that enormously-wonderful mansion in glory? It's time to see as we bring out our first contestant. All the way from Long Beach, California—Testimonial Titan!

T. Titan: Thank you, thank you. My story goes all the way back to my infancy—I was very young then. My mother had agreed to be there at my delivery. Anyway, when I was eight years old, the doctors told my mother that I had only six months to live. That next week, my father ran off with a gypsy fortune-teller. By the time I was ten years old, I was a chain-smoker, but I quickly gave up chains and moved on to cigarettes. Age eleven brought a new birthday cake and a

109

new habit—alcoholism. Soon I was into drugs, first the soft stuff like vitamins, then eventually hard stuff. It was no time at all before I was selling great quantities of hard drugs to little kids on the playground and even to my sixth-grade teacher. I joined the Mafia and also the Black Panthers. I started robbing banks and soaping windows. I fixed the lottery, sold nuclear weapons to the Arabs, and muskets to the Indians. Once I even sold a secret to the Russians, but it was a dumb secret. They didn't know it, though. Then I got into professional athletics. I made it to the Super Bowl twice and to the World Series three times. I was named "Athlete of the Year" several years running, and won five gold medals at the Olympics. Then I joined a rock group and got into witchcraft. And *then* I became a Christian, and it's been precious and wonderful and dynamic ever since. Thank you!

Ernest: Let's hear it for Testimonial Titan! Thank you very much, Titan. That was . . . uh . . . interesting.

Right now we'd like to bring on another wonderful talent from the blessed planet. This young lady has managed to build up a very high level of humility, and she's here to demonstrate. All the way from Toronto, Canada, here's Selena Super-Humble.

Selena: Thank you so much, Ernest. I'd like to make just a simple presentation tonight. Of course, I could go on and on about my credentials for humility—being honored as president eleven years in a row of the Glorious Under-Praised Society of the Humble, or "G.U.S.H." as we called it, and all the Spiritual Awards offered to me which I, of course, turned down. As I told the crowd of 30,000 or so, "I'll get my reward in Heaven." (They loved it!) No, I won't mention these things. Instead I'd like to share with you a song I wrote which I think says it all. It's called "Humility." *(She begins to sing to the tune of "Amazing Grace.")*

(Ernest thinks her song is over and starts to speak after every verse. Finally, Selena finishes.)

Humility, that's what I've got.
You'll see I've got a lot!
I used to be so proud,
I'd brag and boast real loud,
But now my head is bowed.

110

Ernest: Uh . . . thank you, Selena—

I've worked in the church since my early days,
But received no word of praise.
I labored all along,
My name has gone unsung,
I'm sure you'd be amazed.

Ernest: Selena? Thank you—

I gave more than my tithe to the offering plate;
God knows my sacrifice is great.
But I'll not moan and mourn,
I'll never toot my horn,
I just wish to set the record straight.

Ernest *(waits to see if she's finished):* Is that all? Let's hear it for Selena Super-Humble! *(She bows majestically and dramatically again and again.)* Thank you, Selena, thank you. If you'll just go—thank you, Selena, that was fine. Please move over—yes, thank you! *(She finally leaves.)*
　　We've seen some . . . rare talent this evening, and we're looking forward to more. We've got quite a performance coming up next. This young lady has proven her strength time and time again, and tonight she's going to give us a demonstration of that magnificent strength. Here's Tanya, the Temptation Resister!

Tanya: Ladies and gentlemen, allow me to show you a small sampling of the rigid self-discipline and unbelievable self-control which I have been able to build up over years of resisting temptation. First of all, I will demonstrate this strength on an individual basis. Bring on the temptations!

(Tempter #1 comes out as a waiter with a tray of cocktails.)

Tempter #1: Care for a mixed drink, madam?

Tanya *(with indignation):* No!

(Tempter #2 enters walking crazily and carrying a joint.)

Tempter #2: Hey baby, like, you wanna smoke some really fine stuff? It feels *soooo* good!

Tanya: No! *(Turns to audience):* And now I will demonstrate how I react in the face of unexpected temptation—even when no one is around to hear!

(Assistant brings out board with nail and a hammer, then leaves.)

Tanya: Observe. *(She begins to pound nail and "accidentally" hits her thumb. She grabs thumb, looks like she is about to spew out something nasty, then calmly regains control.)* Dear, dear. I believe that I hit my thumb.

(Audience ooohs and aaaahs as assistant comes back out, takes materials and exits).

Tanya: And now I will increase the difficulty of my performance by adding the new dimension of . . . group pressure.

(A raucous mob bursts on stage, all speaking simultaneously.)

Mob: What a great party! I think I'm about out of it! I haven't laughed this much in a long time! Hey, there's Tanya! Hi, Tanya! *(Then, in succession):* Hey Tanya, you want a cigarette? Yeah, you want a smoke, don't ya? Yeah, you wanna be cool, don't ya? Here's cool menthol, filter-tipped! Have one, Tanya! *(They all hold out cigarettes.)*

Tanya: No, thank you, I don't smoke.

Mob *(groans. Then all pull out beer cans, start drinking, and say in succession):* Hey, this Ajax beer is good stuff! Yeah, it's hitting me already! It's mellow and light and hearty! It's a fun beer! Hey, Tanya, you want some Ajax beer? Yeah, go for the gusto! You only go around once! Weekends were made for Ajax! Reach for an Ajax beer! *(All stand with beer can extended toward Tanya.)*

Tanya: No, thank you, I don't drink!

Mob *(groans again, then once more begins talking):* Hey, let's hear a good joke! Yeah, I need a good laugh! Hey, let's make it a dirty joke! Yeah, they're always totally funny! Something really obscene and we'll be in stitches! Hey! Maybe Tanya knows one! Tanya, do you know any really filthy jokes you could tell us? Yeah, c'mon Tanya, tell us a really rank one! Be the laugh of the party! *(They all stand with their heads tilted expectantly.)*

Tanya *(to audience):* Watch this! *(To mob):* No! I don't tell those kind of jokes! *(Mob groans and exits slowly, muttering as they go. Tanya steps forward.)* There you have it! *(She bows victoriously.)*

Ernest: Thank you, Tanya. Thank you very much. Truly a breath-taking performance!
  You may have heard of this next talent. He's got quite a lot of ability and he's eager to show it. Ladies and gentlemen, from Des Moines, Iowa, it's Percy Powerhouse, the Pulpit-Pounding Preacher!

Percy *(in a syrupy preacher's voice):* Ah graciously thank you, Ernest. And folks, remember, eternity is at your doorstep. It's a knock-knock-knockin' at the door of your heart, and it's a rap-tap-tappin' at the cinderblocks in the basement of your stomach. Yes indeed, eternity is lookin' you square in the eye, and let me ask you this question, brothers and sisters, are you prepared to look up? Are you ready to face your eternal destination, whether it be sizzlin' in the fires of endless, torturous perdition, or sashaying down the streets of the Holy City? Amen! But what do you suppose those liberal scholars of our liberal seminaries have to say about the hereafter? What do you suppose those mop-haired, furry-faced, bug-eyed, spectacled eggheads and their crews of ear-tickling, popularity-loving, social-climbing Scripture-rippers have to utter about the afterlife? Do they acknowledge the pearly gates or the key to the blazing abyss? No, no, no! Maybe those cigarette-sucking, cocktail-sippin' compromisers haven't been blessed with any more brains than what would fit in a walnut shell!! Maybe they can't see past their two-inch thick, rose-colored spectacles enough to fix their eyes on what the Holy Scriptures say! One thing for certain, dear people, when those fork-tongued, crowd-pleasin', brainiac apostates in sheep's clothing discover the flames of burnin' sulfur lickin' at their shriveled souls, they're gonna wish with all their hearts that they'd believed the way I do and had come streamin' down the aisle in tears of repentance . . . and tonight, if you'd like to do the same, as we sing all seven verses of "Just As I Am", three times each, hummin' the last verse twice and then singing "Lu-Lu-Lu" on

113

the second verse again, and sing the last verse skipping every other word, you can come—

Ernest *(interrupting):* Uh, Percy, I don't think that's necessary tonight, seeing as how we're in Heaven . . . *(he gestures to the audience).*

Percy *(wiping sweat off his brow):* Oh . . . uh . . . okay.

Ernest: Thank you very much, Percy Powerhouse. Let's give him a big hand!

Percy *(as he exits):* Just say, "Amen"!

Ernest: Our next contestant will, I'm sure, prove to be an impressive performer. From Dallas, Texas, here's Handley Always, the guaranteed healer!

Handley: Watch closely as I demonstrate my uncanny abilities, uh, my uncanny *God-given* abilities to erase from the human form any destructive disorders. First allow me to demonstrate my talents in the realm of internal ailments. The gentleman now entering is suffering from wrenched stomach—tied in a triple, square knot after he accidentally poured Janitor-in-a-Drum on his taco and ate it.

Sickie #1 *(enters holding his stomach, bent over):* Ooooohhh!

Handley: Observe! *(He passes his hand artfully over the sickie's stomach.)* Now you feel it, now you don't.

Sickie #1: Wow! I feel like a million bucks now! And I had to pay only a thousand!

Handley *(puts hand over Sickie's mouth):* Ahem! You may go. *(Louder now):* Next, I will show you my skill at healing inborn blindness.

(Sickie #2 enters with cane and dark sunglasses.)

Handley: Right this way, my good man. *(To audience):* Now watch closely.

Sickie #2: Well, I'll try!

Handley: I was talking to them! *(Waves his hands over sickie's eyes):* Now you don't see it, now you do!

Sickie #2: Ooooh! *(Pause.)* Well, it's still a little dark! *(Handley takes off the man's glasses.)* Wow! There it is! Thank you! Now, where'd you say the collection box was?

(Handley shoves him offstage.)

Handley: And for my final performance—uh, display— uh, *ministry to the sick*, I will heal a terminally crippled person!

(Sickie #3 hobbles out on crutches.)

Handley: Observe my unique "crutch-clutch" method! *(He goes behind the cripple and yanks out his crutches as he exclaims):* Now you've got'em, now you don't!

Sickie #3 *(trying out his "new" legs):* Hey, it worked! Wow, you're pretty good!

Handley: The best! *(Gives crutches back.)* Here! You can use these for clothesline poles! *(To audience):* There you have it! Only a small sample, mind you! *(He bows low.)*

Ernest: Thank you very much Handley! Let's have a big hand for Handley Always, Guaranteed Healer!
　　Our final act this evening is one I'm sure you'll all enjoy—from Oxford University in England, it's Dr. Cyrus Rote, ace Bible scholar!

Cyrus *(enters to applause, carrying scroll):* Much gratitude, much gratitude. At this vespertinal moment, I relish the opportunity to deliver to you a minimal representation of my years and years and years of intense Scriptural rumination. It is my immense pleasure to share with this esteemed configuration only a few of the more enthralling, most enlightening passages from a few of my research scrolls. *(He reads wordy, academic excerpts glued inside the scrolls in droning monotone until Ernest finally has to cut him off.)*

Ernest: Uh, excuse me, Dr. Rote, but we'll have to bring this to a close. You've already overwhelmed us with your vast knowledge.

Cyrus: Oh . . . much gratitude, much gratitude. *(He exits.)*

Ernest: Well everyone, the moment of truth has finally arrived. Which contestant has earned that unspeakably glorious mansion in the Holy City? Which one has truly shown himself or herself to be worthy of the grand award? I believe our Judge is ready with a decision, so if our six contestants will step out, I will reveal the contents of the Judge's envelope! Contestants, I'm sure you're anxious to find out who is the winner, who has shined the brightest with spiritual qualities, who is the Star of Heaven? The envelope please . . . *(he opens it)*. And the winner is, . . . none of the contestants! *(The contestants gasp and exclaim in disbelief.)* But wait! Here's the Judge's explanation: "Most think that the big points are scored on stage in the spotlight, but My cameras were always on—backstage as well as onstage. True spirituality is not measured by how you perform, but by how you live." *(Contestants, with their heads hung low, begin to slowly exit, one by one.)* "For even if you speak powerful testimonies, or appear to be humble, or resist temptations, or preach mighty sermons, or heal the sick, or possess all knowledge, but have not love, you have done nothing."

Well, I'm sure our contestants have learned that the Stars of Heaven are those who love. And for the rest of you, that mansion is still waiting . . . not for those with impressive performances, but impressive lives. Thank you and good night!

Curtain

What to Do On a Date

Characters
Mark Smith, strong, young Christian, a little shy
JoJo Flop, a flamboyant teen boy, acts cool, doesn't listen to
anyone
Bernice Flop, a nice, blond girl
Mamma Flop, somewhat airheaded

Setting
The Flop living room.

Props/Costumes
A couch, or several chairs in a row to simulate one
A blond wig for Bernice, if needed

Performance Tips

The argument between Mark and JoJo does not have to be heated, but should be strong enough to convey the message. If Bernice is not played by a blond, cut the Goldilocks line.

Scene: *Audience hears a knock on the door as curtains open. Mama Flop opens the door and invites Mark into the house.*

Mamma Flop: Well come in, Mark, come on in.

Mark *(entering the room):* Thank you, Mrs. Flop.

Mamma Flop: How's your job down at the shoelace factory?

Mark: Just fine, ma'am.

Mamma Flop: Well, there's nothing like summertime when you're young! You can work those crazy, part-time jobs, get a lot of time off, lay in the sun, drink pop, go swimming and have a blast!

Mark *(sadly):* Mrs. Flop, my father's been layed off from his job and I have to work about a hundred hours a week to support the family. I don't get much time off, my eyes are sensitive to the sun, my stomach can't take the acids in soft drinks, and I almost drowned when I was little, so I never go near water.

Mamma Flop *(slowly, unbelieving):* Well, I'm sorry to hear that, Mark.

Mark *(happier):* How's *your* job at the staple gun factory, Mrs. Flop?

Mamma Flop: Oh, it's business as usual—everything's real "together." *(Laughs at her own joke.)*

Mark *(happy for her):* Yeah, right.

(JoJo enters the house just as Bernice enters from another room.)

JoJo *(very energetic):* Hey, everybody! What's happenin'? Mark, glad you could see me!

Bernice: Hi, Mark.

JoJo *(speaking to Bernice):* Hey, sister Goldilocks, life must be a bear! *(Laughs at his own joke.)*

Bernice: I can't believe you stole Harold's car from school and took it to the mall!

JoJo *(not listening to her):* Hey everybody, you should have seen me today! I stole Harold Barkdog's car and took it to the mall!

Bernice: Harold's comin' to get you.

JoJo *(doesn't listen):* Hey Ma, it's good to see me!

Bernice *(to JoJo):* Oh, you never listen! *(To Mark):* I'll be back in a minute. *(She leaves the stage and Mark sits down on the couch.)*

Mamma Flop: JoJo, it's not nice to steal other boys' cars.

JoJo *(not listening, walks over to Mark):* Hey Mark, nice shoes.

Mamma Flop: You're gonna end up in jail eating bugs for protein.

JoJo *(sits down next to Mark):* Listen to this. *(points to Mamma):* She'll probably tell me I'm gonna end up in jail eating bugs for protein! *(Looks at Mamma expectantly, but she leaves the room. JoJo shrugs his shoulders.)* Oh well. So Mark, what are you doing here?

Mark: Well, I . . .

JoJo: Hey, I bet I know! You're here because you heard that I give excellent advice about what to do on a date!

Mark *(shaking head "no"):* Well, I . . .

JoJo: Are you interested in some girl?

Mark: Well, as a matter of fact, yes.

JoJo *(leans back confidently, puts hands behind his head):* Do you know what to do on a date?

Mark: Not exactly.

JoJo *(sits back up excitedly)*: Where do you want to take this chick?

Mark: To a movie.

JoJo: Excellent! That's a good choice because you don't have to talk to her. *(Slight pause.)* Now, you'll want to go to a really scary movie.

Mark: Why?

JoJo *(unbelieving)*: Why? Where have you been? You take a girl to a scary movie so she will get scared all over ya.

Mark: You mean throw up on me? I don't know if I want . . .

JoJo: No, no! Get brains, dude! So she will cuddle up to you.

Mark *(looks around uneasily)*: Oh. I don't know, I . . .

JoJo: You're probably saying to yourself, "What if she doesn't scare easy and she won't cuddle up to me?" Well, I have lots of ways to start the ball rollin'. You've got to put your arm around her. Picture this; you're sitting there in the theater watching the movie. *(Moves close to Mark.)* You're not talking—that's good—but you want to put your arm around her. Try the "JoJo lint" routine.

Mark: The lint routine?

JoJo: Yeah! Just say, "Oh! It looks like you've got a little lint on your shoulder." *(Puts his arm around Mark and picks at his shoulder.)* See how easy it is? Then you've got to kiss her.

Mark *(looking around, very uneasy)*: Hey, I don't know . . .

JoJo: All you have to say is, "Mmmmm, your lips sure look good! I bet they taste good, too. Let me try." *(Leans over like he's going to kiss Mark.)*

Mark *(gets up in a hurry)*: Hey! Whoa, whoa, whoa! I get the point!

JoJo: I wasn't gonna plant one on ya; get sick! But you get the idea, right? Listen man, if you don't get a little, you ain't been on a date! After the kiss and after the movie, you can go on to other things! *(Elbowing him.)* If ya know what I mean!

Mark: JoJo, That's not right. I like to treat a girl like a lady. I'm a Christian and I think God wants us to do other things on a date besides trying to "get a little." What about talking, getting to know each other?

JoJo: Ah, that's for nerds! I'm telling you, you've got to get a little something from her. Guys pay for the date, they deserve something in return. The girls should pay up—they should go all the way.

Mark: All the way where? We're only going to the movie!

JoJo: Oh come on! You know what I mean!

Mark: You bet I do! And sex isn't "all the way!" You go farther with a girl when you start caring about each other, learn to laugh together, and feel comfortable praying together. I don't expect to be "paid back!" After all, I asked her out; she didn't ask me.

JoJo: Hey man, the way girls dress today—they *want* to get us all heated up!

Mark: Well, it does seem that way sometimes. But the same thing is true with the guys, too. Besides, the Lord has told us that sex before marriage is wrong.

JoJo *(very sarcastically):* Ahhhh, I can tell *you're* a Christian! You Christians are all alike; you make sex out to be a dirty thing. But when two people love each other, the need to show their love in the deepest way.

Mark: And how may girls will you "love" before you get married?

JoJo *(dismissing him):* Ahhh!

Mark: Christians don't make sex out to be a dirty thing. I think its such a beautiful thing that I'm saving it for the person I marry. That's the way God wants it. He want sex to be special and lifelong. *And,* he want us to see our dates as His children, girls who are precious in His sight.

JoJo: Ah, what difference does it make whose child she is? If she's a babe, she's made for kissin'. I still say, go out with this girl you like and go for it. (Mark shakes his head sadly.) So who's the babe you want to go out with anyway?

Mark: Bernice, your sister.

JoJo *(jumps up from the couch in anger):* What!? You want to go out with *my* sister?! You want to take my sister to the *movies?* You want to lock lips with *my sister?* You want to go all the way with my *sister?!*

Mark *(stands up and holds his hand up to JoJo):* Whoa! You said all that stuff, not me!

JoJo *(suddenly changes and becomes very nice to Mark):* Hey, listen! You've got some *great* ideas about dating! You ought to stick with *every* one of them! *(Puts his arm around Mark's shoulders.)* Let's go to the kitchen and find something to eat, and we'll talk some more, okay? *(Starts walking Mark out of the room.)* I'll tell you about a nice restaurant you can take Bernice to. . . .

(They walk off.)

Curtain

Where Have You Been?

Characters
Mike, an older teen, thoughtful, kind
David, a younger brother, rebellious but basically good
Parents, average parents
Voice, plays T.V. voice and policeman on phone

Setting
A living room.

Props/Costumes
Window
Couch or chairs
T.V.
Telephone
Magazines
Prerecorded sounds of car moving past house and telephone
    ringing

Performance Tips
A real window is not necessary but will add to the performance. The voice over the phone can be done by someone off-stage with a cup at the side of the mouth to simulate an

over-the-phone sound. Dave needs to take his time with the actions that show he is growing scared. Dave's thinking to himself can be done with another voice over the PA for added effect.

Scene: *Mike is watching television, Dave sneaks in the front door and glides behind Mike's chair (or couch).*

Dave *(pops up behind Mike, whispers):* Pssssst! Mike! Where are Mom and Dad?

Mike *(loud, mocking whisper):* They're gone. *(Slow and distinct):* The coast is clear!

Dave *(speaks freely):* Oh, good! *(Sits down.)* I never mean to be late.

Mike *(looking at T.V.):* Yes, you do.

Dave *(unconcerned):* You're right. So where's the night patrol?

Mike *(correcting and looking at Dave):* Mom and Dad are out for a romantic evening; dinner and something else after that.

Dave: Great! Just as long as they're not here to catch me and get all over me.

Mike *(sarcastically):* Right.

Dave *(looking at the television):* What's on?

Mike *(caring, sad):* A news break. Somebody murdered a boy.

Dave *(uncaring):* Another day, another murder in the news, huh?

Mike: Dave, that boy was somebody's son, maybe somebody's brother; think about how those people feel. *(Both are looking at the T.V.)*

Dave: They don't look like they are all that crazy about it. They probably won't go bowling tonight.

Mike: No, really, it's got to be horrible for them.

Dave *(sarcastically):* I don't see what the big deal is about death. Everybody is gonna die. I don't think all that crying and blubbering is necessary. People should expect death and face it.

Mike *(a little angry):* I don't think it's as easy as that. How could you or I judge? We've never experienced death.

Dave *(laughs):* It's kind of hard to talk about death after it happens to you.

Mike: You know what I mean. We've never lost anybody close to us, who really mattered in our lives.

Dave: Still, everybody knows that everybody dies. *(Pauses to think, says uncaringly):* People should just forget the dead.

Mike *(sarcastically):* Oh, that's great! *(Gets up to turn off T.V.)* I can see you walking up to this kid's parents *(points to the T.V.)* saying "So, your kid is dead. You've loved him, cherished him, had great hopes for his life, but suddenly at the tender age of seven, *(with emphasis)* somebody shoots him! *(Mocks Dave's uncaring attitude):* He's dead, but don't worry, I have the answer; just forget him!" And I'm sure the parents are going to say, "Oh, thanks! We never thought of that; let's go bowling!"

Dave *(unsure of himself):* That's not exactly what I meant.

Mike *(still a little angry):* Well, what do you mean?

Dave *(somewhat frustrated):* I don't know.

Mike *(thinks for a moment and then asks):* How would you feel if Mom and Dad died?

Dave *(looks around, thinking, replies without much feeling):* I, I guess I wouldn't be laughing. I'm not sure.

Mike: No, really. They've been hanging around us all of our lives. How would it feel if they weren't around anymore?

Dave *(defensively):* It hasn't been all that great having them around! Because of them, I have to sneak into my own house!

Mike *(not believing Dave's attitude):* You wouldn't have to sneak in if you came home when they ask you!

Dave *(gets up to defend himself):* How about last month when they got all over me? Remember that Saturday night they told me to be in at 12:00? They grounded me for coming in an hour early!

Mike *(trying to be reasonable):* David, you came home on Sunday.

Dave: So?

Mike: You were twenty-three hours late.

Dave *(faking a defense):* Now, uh, that's what I mean; they're on my case every single day!

Mike *(with more intensity):* Oh, now, are they really? You just don't know how much of their lives they've sacrificed for you. I remember, like it was yesterday, standing there watching Mom change your diapers. Do you remember that?

Dave: No, not really.

Mike *(grimaces):* It was disgusting! *(Pauses to think.)* Do you remember the time you tried to dry your pants in the oven and you caught them on fire? Mom pulled you away and she burnt her hand!

Dave: Yeah, *(thinks):* but they beat me for that one!

Mike: Dave, they *spanked* you! And you learned your lesson, didn't you? And how about the time your car broke down on the way to the prom? Mom and Dad skipped that adult sweetheart banquet at church to take you and your date to the dance.

Dave *(remembering with feeling):* Yeah, that was neat! Dad showed up in a hat and a black suit and opened the door for us, like a chauffeur; that was great!

Mike *(with deeper feeling):* Remember that Christmas when Dad was laid off?

Dave *(very serious):* We thought we weren't going to get any presents.

Mike: But when we came downstairs on Christmas morning, there were two bikes next to the tree. *(Points to a place in the room where the tree was.)*

Dave *(looking down, feeling ashamed):* We found out later that they had to borrow money for those bikes. They didn't have to do that.

Mike *(looking for Dave's reaction):* It would have been enough just to be together.

Dave *(thinking):* Yeah.

Mike *(after a pause):* So—how *would* you feel if Mom and Dad died?

Dave *(trying without luck to hide his feelings):* Man, I don't even want to think about it! *(Lowers his head.)*

Mike *(smiles and nods his head):* Well—I think I'll hit the sack; I'm beat. Mom and Dad should . . . *(checks his watch)* hum-mmm . . . they're an hour late. Must be having a good time. *(Walks over to edge of stage.)*

Dave *(a little worried, looks at his watch):* Think I'll stay up for a while.

Mike: Okay. Night. *(Leaves the stage.)*

Dave: *(picks up a magazine, flips a few pages, looks at his watch, flips a few more pages, looks at watch again, then puts the magazine down.)*

(PA: Sound of a car approaching.)

Dave: *(goes to window to see if car is his parents.' It's not. He sits down and thinks out loud):* I wonder where Mom and Dad are? *(Pause.)* They've never been late before.

(Gets up and turns on the T.V.)
T.V. Voice: "It's late, do you know where your parents are?"

Dave: *(quickly, nervously—turns off the T.V and leans over it, breathing heavily. Goes back to couch and sits down, tries to relax. The phone rings, scaring him, and he picks it up quickly.)*

Dave *(anxiously):* Hello?

Voice on phone: Is this the Hampton residence?

Dave *(nervously):* Yes, yes it is.

Voice: This is the *(name of your city)* police department. I'm afraid we have some bad news for you.

Dave *(nervously):* Yes, what is it?

Voice: There's been an accident *(pause)* involving death. *(Long pause.)*

Dave *(whispering, choking):* What. . . who . . .?

Voice: Do you own a cocker spaniel?

Dave *(delayed reaction):* Yes—yes we do. *(Pause.)* What? He's been hit by a car? *He's* dead? That's great! Thanks for calling me! *(He hangs up the phone just as his parents walk in.)*

Dave *(very excited):* Mom and Dad! *(Stops, looks at his watch and gets angry.)* Where have you been!? You're over an hour late! I've been worried sick about you!

(Parents, perplexed try to answer, but are cut off.)

Dave *(helpless, almost crying):* The police called; the dog's dead. *(Anger turns to relief):* It sure is good to see you! *(Throws his arms around his parents. Dave's back is to the audience.)*

(While being hugged, parents look at each other over or around Dave and look totally baffled.)

Curtain